# The Finding Properties Toolbox:

Buying Real Estate at a Discount

By

Quentin D'Souza

The Finding Properties Toolbox:
Buying Real Estate at a Discount
Copyright © 2022 DREIC Publishing

The information in this book is provided for information purposes and intended to be general guidelines only. It is not legal, financial, tax, insurance, or accounting advice. Such advice may only be given by a licensed professional. It is just the author's opinion.

Publisher: DREIC Publishing

Copyright Canada, USA, and the World 2022

Feedback and Comments: info@findingdiscountedproperties.com

More Information – www.FindingDiscountedProperties.com

ISBN: 978-0-9936717-5-3

# The Finding Properties Toolbox:

Buying Real Estate at a Discount

By
Quentin D'Souza

# Contents

Acknowledgements . . . . . . . . . . . . . . . . . . . . . . . vii

Introduction . . . . . . . . . . . . . . . . . . . . . . . . . . . ix

Chapter 1: Setting the Stage . . . . . . . . . . . . . . . . . 1

Chapter 2: Becoming a Geographic Specialist . . . . . . . . 9

Chapter 3: Driving in Your Area . . . . . . . . . . . . . . . 13

Chapter 4: Using Some Data to Help You Take Action . . . . 17

Chapter 5: Setting Up a Voicemail System . . . . . . . . . 27

Chapter 6: Finding Discounted Properties
Takes Time and Money. . . . . . . . . . . . . . 31

Chapter 7: Leveraging Real Estate Agents
(Your Power Team). . . . . . . . . . . . . . . . 37

Chapter 8: The Multiple Listing Service (MLS) . . . . . . . 45

Chapter 9: For Sale by Owner. . . . . . . . . . . . . . . . 53

Chapter 10: Private Sales . . . . . . . . . . . . . . . . . . 59

Chapter 11: Focusing on a Specific Area . . . . . . . . . . 71

Chapter 12: Wholesalers . . . . . . . . . . . . . . . . . . 85

Chapter 13: The Lead Sheet . . . . . . . . . . . . . . . . 97

Chapter 14: Offline Print Marketing. . . . . . . . . . . . .103

Chapter 15: Online Marketing. . . . . . . . . . . . . . . .109

Chapter 16: Online Marketing. . . . . . . . . . . . . . . .119

Chapter 17: Creating Equity from Emails.. . . . . . . . . .127

Chapter 18: Dealing Directly with Potential Sellers.. . . . .129

Chapter 19: Leveraging Your Network . . . . . . . . . . .135

Chapter 20: Get Outside of the Box . . . . . . . . . . . .143

Chapter 21: Car-Based Advertising . . . . . . . . . . . . .147

Chapter 22: Bandit Signs . . . . . . . . . . . . . . . . . .151

Chapter 23: Stickers . . . . . . . . . . . . . . . . . . . . .157

Chapter 24:  Door Hangers, Flyers, or Postcards . . . . . .161

Chapter 25: Business Cards . . . . . . . . . . . . . . . . .165

Chapter 26: Other Ideas. . . . . . . . . . . . . . . . . . .169

    Dialing for Dollars . . . . . . . . . . . . . . . . . . . .169

    Walking Billboard . . . . . . . . . . . . . . . . . . . .170

Chapter 27: Conclusion . . . . . . . . . . . . . . . . . . .171

Suggested Reading . . . . . . . . . . . . . . . . . . . . .173

Author Biography – Quentin D'Souza . . . . . . . . . . . .175

# Acknowledgements

I started writing this book during the pandemic in 2021 and completed it in 2022. There were many people that helped me throughout the process. I'd like to start by thanking DurhamREI members and EducationREI members for giving me feedback on the numerous handouts and video training that I produce for members.

I'd like to thank my wife Laura, for listening to me talk real estate in the evening, on weekends and every other time when she would rather not hear about a tenant, deal, house or apartment building. Her support means the world to me.

I want to encourage my two sons – Darcy and Lucas to use this book to help them to achieve their financial goals and grow a real estate portfolio for themselves.

I wanted to thank Aaron Moore, Michael Chow, Rick & Don Lewis, Michael Lee, Luc Boiron, Tony Peters, Andrew Brennan, Michael Dominguez, Sarah Rayfield, Amit Dey and many others who helped bring the idea to life with direct help, indirect support or sharing resources.

Finally, I wanted to thank the many accredited investors that I have worked with over the last decade and wanted to thank them for their trust in me, and I wanted to congratulate them on their real estate investing success. We have built an amazing portfolio of real estate together.

# Introduction

## Off Market and Discounted Properties: Real Estate System

The purpose of this book is to help you find off market opportunities. Sometimes, the benefit of finding an off market opportunity means that you are not competing with 100 other people for the same property. Sometimes, it is solving people's problems in other ways, and by offering them a solution, you are able to buy the property at a discount. This is one of the many ways to find discounted properties. There are countless great investment opportunities out there, but we need you to be a great real estate investor so that you can find them. All of the information is great that is out there, but you need to do the actions mentioned in this book that will help you to succeed.

Using this book, doing the actions and using this experience that keeps building up as you go through the chapters will help you to succeed at finding off market and discounted properties. Remember, this book is full of tips, information, and documents—essentially everything you need to find off market opportunities. Each chapter contains unique information that will help you to find future deals.

So, if you are ready to grow your portfolio, then this is just the book for you. We are going to look at marketing strategies for off market properties. We are going to do some number crunching around evaluating deals. We are going to talk about determining the right purchase price. We are going to learn about the right techniques that will help you to create equity out of your deals, how to target the right properties, and the sellers that are willing to give you the best deals. So, that is our goal for this book. Now, how are we going to do that? Well, we have a roadmap that is going to help you do that—we are going to look at setting the stage, becoming a geographic expert, looking at an area, trigger points, voicemail, MLS, private sales, specific wholesalers marketing, and the list goes on and on.

We have a lot going on here in this book, and I cannot wait for you to get started. So, big picture, we are thinking about it in different sections. First, we are going to focus on understanding off market opportunities, what they are, how they work, and how you can use them to grow your portfolio. In the next section, we are going to talk about building an off market system—you need deal flow. Without deal flow, you are not going to get your next deal. Then, we are going to focus on the marketing system. Once you have built it, we are going to use it and utilize that off market system. Finally, we are going to look at thinking outside the box and getting the deal done.

This course is a book full of strategies, tips, information, and documents that are designed to help you find off market properties.

Each chapter contains actions that will help you find unique future real estate deals. There is a lot of work involved, but if you are ready to grow your portfolio, then this is the book for you.

- **Strategies for marketing specifically** for off market properties.
- **Strategies for crunching the numbers and evaluating deals** to create high-profit margins.
- **Learning to determine the right purchase price.**
- **Learning to use the right techniques** that will help you create equity when you purchase.
- **Learning how to target the right properties** and the sellers that will give you the best deals.

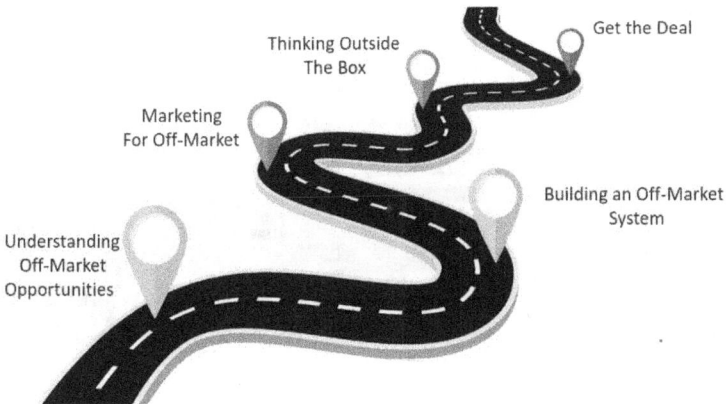

Thinking Outside The Box

Get the Deal

Marketing For Off-Market

Building an Off-Market System

Understanding Off-Market Opportunities

# Chapter 1

# Setting the Stage

The purpose of this book is to help you to find off market deals. There are plenty of opportunities out there, but make sure you take the actions that are being shared here.

Sometimes investors don't realize the power of taking a property and changing it into something that will make it an extremely good deal.

- **Adding a Bedroom**
- **Adding a Secondary Suite**
- **Renting out a Garage, Shed, or Storage**
- **Doing a Top Up**
- **Changing the Use**
- **Minor Variance**
- **And More**

These are skills that you can learn if you take the time to develop them.

Sometimes investors do not realize the power of taking a property and transforming it into something that could turn it into an exceptionally good deal. When you are looking at a property, you see that they have converted a bedroom into a dining room, but it makes more sense as a rental property to convert it back into a bedroom. That way, instead of having two bedrooms upstairs, you have three bedrooms upstairs. Things as simple as that can significantly increase the yield on a property. Renting a two-bedroom upstairs may give you, let us say $1,600, even with a large dining room and living room, but having three bedrooms upstairs might give you $1,800. It is just as simple as that. It can also be taking a single-family home and adding a secondary suite. Sometimes, adding a secondary suite does not mean a basement apartment—that could be a vertical split, which means a split on the top and basement unit down the middle if it is a bungalow. A secondary unit could be created through an addition on the back as well. There are a lot of different ways to do it.

It could be, renting out a garage that is separate from the unit, or renting out a shed or a storage area to another person, meaning that you will increase the yield that you are getting from that property. It could be taking a bungalow and adding a second floor onto it and the square footage would make that property double, and because of the way that you purchased the property, the value increases to an extent that it makes sense to sell as a flip or hold on to it.

Perhaps, you are changing the use of the property. Maybe you are in Toronto, Canada and you are buying a single-family home for $800,000 or a million dollars that may not be cash flow positive. However, if you are able to take it and, perhaps, have two suites in the basement, you have turned that single-family home into an easy triplex. I always advocate for that to be a legal change. Changing the use could mean going to the town and doing a zoning change, moving it from single-family zoning to something that is a higher density. Therefore, by just doing that, you are adding value to the land, aside from the building on top of it. You could even sell the land to a developer to do a larger development on.

Perhaps, what you need to do is understand the area and do a minor variance to give you the parking requirement necessary in order to do a legal secondary suite. There are tons of different ways that you can do this in order to take a property and turn it into a great deal. These are skills that you will learn over time. You can learn them from other people and from books like this. However, you should always remember, this is not a sprint, it is a marathon. It is about learning and applying and being able to grow your portfolio.

## Work Harder and Smarter to Find Good Deals

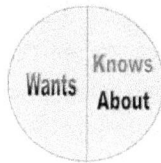

| Properties that nobody wants | Wants / Knows About | Properties that people don't know about |

Let us talk about working harder and smarter to find good deals. The good deals are out there; they are either the properties that nobody wants or properties that nobody knows about. So, a property that nobody wants could be something that smells like cat pee, a hoarder house, had a fire—something that is a lot harder for people to deal with; perhaps, even rough tenants. Those are properties that nobody wants. The properties that nobody knows about are people who want to sell but have not listed them on the MLS, but they do want to sell. If you look at the type of properties that I have bought over the years, just in the MLS, for instance, in order to find the discount, it usually runs in one of those two categories. When you are looking for properties that are off market, they could be properties that nobody wants, as well as properties that people do not know about, or a combination of the two.

Now, when we talk about motivated sellers, what does that mean? Firstly, it means, you understand their motivation to sell. Is there a specific problem that you can solve with your offer? Many people try and use different strategies to negotiate and try to be very non-confrontational, but really, negotiating is about the relationship with the person that you are dealing with, and it will often take you out of your comfort zone. That is why people work with realtors, because that is what they do. A good realtor should be somebody who negotiates for you, but if you are not going to use a realtor, then you need to improve your negotiation skills. This can give you a real advantage, and you can use strategies that realtors cannot use because you are not bound by a license like them. Now, if you are a realtor, and you are reading this, you have other advantages that an investor does not have, which is usually related to access to the MLS, although that is starting to change. We will talk about different tools that investors can access.

I have found that people are willing to give up equity in return for you to solve the problem that they are facing. They will be thankful to have found you, despite what some people will tell you. I found that, unfortunately, it is realtors that usually say, *"You are taking advantage of people because they are giving up equity."* I think that appears to be from somebody who is probably jealous. It is always solving a problem that somebody else has, and you are trying to help them do this as quickly as possible. In order to help them, you need something for that, just like a realtor is not selling your property for free. They are getting paid for the transaction, and you are getting paid for this transaction by solving a difficult problem.

## Know Your Reasons Why

**There are many others aspects of Real Estate Investing that will contribute to your success:**

- **Development of your team**
- **Understanding the economic fundamentals of the area**
- **Running your rental properties like a little business**
- **Filling vacancies and much more.**

Why do you need to know your reason? Why? Well, there are many other aspects to real estate investing that will contribute to your success at finding off market properties. So, why are you doing this? Are you developing an amazing house flip or development team? Do you want to create a business? Are you working on developing a team of people as well and want to contribute to their success? As for who is going to be on that team, you will have realtors, mortgage brokers, private lenders, appraisers, inspectors, and contractors. So, you are going to be developing all of those relationships.

The other thing that you need to know is why are you investing in that particular area? It is great that you have a marketing campaign, and I hear about people who have marketing campaigns all over the province or the country. So, why are you doing it? Are you being transactional? Are you treating real estate like you are day trading stocks? Well, that is great in hot markets, but it does not always work.

That is probably when you should be doing flips in a hot market, but you have to understand the fundamentals in the area because what happens is your legs get cut right out from under you. When the market shifts, and it will shift quickly, you could get stuck with a property that does not make financial sense. Therefore, understand the economic fundamentals of the area. What does a cash flowing property look like? Where is that area in the real estate cycle? Remember that even when we are talking about finding discounted properties, we want to run our rental properties like it is a business. The same thing with how we fill our vacancies and much more—we want to know why we are doing these things? How does that fit into the bigger picture?

**You always need to consider before any purchase – is this bringing me closer to my goals and the reason why I am investing in real estate?**

Most of the time, people who buy real estate are buying it because they have heard about huge appreciation, passive income, getting rich quickly. Be careful with the idea that it is easy to make money in real estate. I want to rephrase that. It is simple to make money in real estate but it certainly is not easy. The idea here is that you want to consider the real reason for purchasing that real estate. Do you want to create a different type of lifestyle for yourself? Do you want to create freedom for yourself? Where do you want to be in the buying process? Are you just creating another job for yourself? If that is the case, maybe instead of being the active partner, you should be the passive partner in a real estate deal. Perhaps you want to add properties to your portfolio, but adding a single-family home in a nice area is going to be a lot easier for you to handle and be part of your lifestyle than managing a triplex in a really tough area, where you may be able to get some additional cash flow. Are you willing to deal with the issues that come up?

Even if you have a property manager on the property, you are still going to have to deal with those issues. Remember, there are some lifestyle choices for all of us when investing in real estate. Keep this in mind as I am reiterating it again, know your reason!

Why are you finding these properties? That mindset piece is key! Now, you will need to consider a lot of things before any purchase, but one thing I suggest, is to ask yourself if this property brings me closer to my real estate or financial goals? Is it bringing me closer to the reason why I am investing in real estate? This can be asked by you when you find an off market property. It can be a part of your decision, why you hold that in your portfolio, and/or why you end up selling it and then perhaps flipping it. It could be the rule, "*I do not hold condos in my portfolio.*" So, your plan A is to flip that property, and then your plan B is to hold it as a rental. You need to be certain if this next purchase or this property is bringing me towards my goals or away from my goals. What is that goal? You are going to have to outline what that is.

Consider writing a letter to yourself as if you were writing from your future self to your present self. I want you to describe what your life looks like one year from now. What does it look like three years from now? What does it look like ten years from now? The idea is to use this reflection to plan your life more than you plan a vacation. If you can do that and can use a simple tool like this, then I think you will be much better off in the long run. This is just giving you the mindset—the piece that will help you the most. I know, it does not seem like it, but it is the mindset that is going to help you get through some of the tough times, get through different negotiations, get through purchasing a property, and some of the trials and tribulations that happen when you are dealing with real estate and people.

# Chapter 2

# Becoming a Geographic Specialist

I really want to focus on the importance of becoming an area geographic specialist, rather than having a shotgun type of approach. Marketing everywhere is impractical and does not really get you anywhere quickly. I want you to start with your local area, and then expand outwards into other areas once you have developed your expertise. Remember, you are always developing a team as you go along. It is not about getting into every Facebook real estate group and putting your name out there or creating a handful of buyer's lists for people that you are never going to interact with. This is about focusing, becoming a specialist, and then developing good strong relationships with people as you go along.

- **Start with Your Local Area**
- **Expand Outwards to New Areas**
- **Develop a Team as You Go Along**

When you become a geographic specialist, the lowest purchase price goal should never be the sole reason why you buy a property. There are lots of other reasons to pursue a property. For example, the renovations needed for the property could actually bring you well above that low purchase price. It could be because of foundation issues, maybe there is a zoning problem, or there is something problematic with the land that you are buying. You need to be methodical, and a low purchase price should never be the only motivation for you to buy something, as then you might not be able to reap the rewards.

## Low purchase price should never be the sole reason to buy a property

**For Example:**

- The renovations that you might need to do to the property could bring you well above market price.
- There might be an additional opportunity, through two pieces of land beside each other.
- You can reposition tenants in a multi-unit building with extreme value increase

There might be an additional opportunity when it comes to this. If you have two pieces of land beside each other and, perhaps, buying one for a little bit more could be a great decision because you own the property beside it. Or if it is a multifamily building, and although the rents are quite low, the purchase price could be a bit higher, but you can get a lot of additional value by repositioning the tenants and turning over the tenants in that building so the value of the building goes up even more. There are aspects other than the price point that should be taken into consideration for any purchase that you do.

- Licensing Areas
- Flood Zones
- Student Rental Areas
- A,B,C Tenant Areas

- **Methadone Clinics**
- **Ability to Add Secondary Suites**
- **Ability to Add Garden Suites**
- **Understanding Zoning**

When you become a geographic specialist, you start to understand what is happening in different areas, as all across Ontario. In some municipalities, you have licensed areas. So, in order to rent a property, you may have to have a license and oftentimes there is an annual inspection. Quite frankly, that is almost to the point of bureaucratic absurdity and a money grab; it is ridiculous and a duplication of services like property standards/by-law enforcement.

You have to watch out for flood zones to keep your investment safe. If you are not familiar with an area and you do not know who to call to find out whether a property is in a flood zone, it could be a problem. In North America, there are usually different environmental agencies that make flood plain information public. For example, in my area I would use the Central Lake Ontario Conservation Authority Floodplain mapping tool.

What if it is in the student's rental area and you didn't know about it? This could affect your appraisals later on or affect your intentions on what to do with the property. Instead of flipping the property to an end buyer, perhaps, you would need to focus on selling it to a parent or a student, or an investor.

Maybe you do not know whether that is a Class A, Class B, or Class C tenant profile property. We do not really have Class D in Ontario, which would be like a war zone. And you think you are going to get a higher property price on sale but because of the tenant profile it drags down the sale price.

Is the property beside a methadone clinic? Are they going to have a different type of tenant profile, to put it politely? If you are buying beside a methadone clinic, knowing the area is important. That is why if you are just posting ads everywhere and you are not sure where you are investing in, it is going to be more challenging later on.

While with time, you will start to get the hang of it and things become easier. In the beginning, you need to be mindful of these factors. Can you add secondary suites? Can you add garden suites? What is the zoning like? What is it like working and dealing with the town or city? I want you to be aware of these factors when you are looking at a property. It is not just about the actual purchase price of the property; there can be other reasons and you need to know that.

# Chapter 3

# Driving in Your Area

I am going to give you a couple of tips here. I want you to think about driving in the area that you want to focus on. Specifically, if you are just getting started, I want you to focus on a local area. You cannot do everything from behind your computers—it is not going to bring any results. You need to talk to other investors, you need to go out for lunch or dinner, or go out on the weekends and talk to them. You need to find out which properties are cash flowing, where are they cash flowing, and what properties do they own. In particular, listen to what street they purchase on. Did it cash flow well when they purchased it? Does it cash flow well at today's purchase price? What streets are the majority of investors purchasing on? You need to take the time to do the research.

A simple trick is to research the locations simply by just looking them up on Kijiji and seeing where they are located. Where are the properties? What types of properties are available that are being listed for rent at?

Then, you need to identify the housing types that you are interested in purchasing. You should know if they are detached houses, semi-detached houses, townhouses, condos, or apartment buildings—what are they? What are you going to invest in? You should have that idea and then when you are clear, you are going to be able to identify streets where these houses are located. What you can do is take a notebook and list all of the streets, perhaps, have your phone with you. Just make sure that you focus on the areas that you want to purchase in. You can even get one of those old paper maps and you can highlight the different streets that you want to look at, and then go visit those desired streets. You want to check out the area. Is it safe to get out of your car? You want to probably visit at different times during the day and especially on the weekend.

The reason why you should plan to visit on the weekends is so that you can hopefully see more people. On the contrary, you see fewer people on a working day when you know they are away working. If you are looking at starter homes, are you noticing lots of cars in the driveway during the day on a weekday? It will tell you about what is going on and what their employment prospects are—something that could be noticeably different nowadays because of telecommuting and the virtual meetings. However, it is categorically something that you want to consider, particularly when you are thinking about an area. You also want to know the pertinent stuff that you like about the area, such as an elementary school, high school, shopping malls, parks—which are part of the area where the property is located. The same is the case with Community Centers and other things of public interest for renting a property or selling a property.

You need to identify what are those benefits that you cannot really change in a property because it is located in a particular area. Looking back at when I was traveling to the US to find areas to invest in, I rented a car for a few days and drove through the different areas. I visited a local real estate investment club and I talked to people who were there, and I tried to find out different areas, met with realtors, and visited properties. These are all ways I used to develop a better understanding of different areas I am interested in. Am I an expert at that city or town yet? No, but I am learning and I am getting there. I am spending the time to do it. I did the same thing when I started where I invest locally. I visited areas and I lived in the area, but I still didn't know all of the different streets until I started to visit them. So, you have to take the time and get that expertise. You can always grow that into different areas as you become more familiar with the process, but it is a mistake to go right into a shotgun approach to look at properties across a large area rather than focus on a few streets.

Now, what about if you are driving the area and you see a property that you want to make an offer on? Here is a simple tip. While you are driving, you should always have a sticky notepad or a notecard with you. Create something simple like a template for a handwritten note to leave at the house that you are interested in purchasing. We will go into templates a little bit later on, but I will give you something minimal and you can go to a place like Vistaprint to create something effortlessly. Make sure that you put a sticky note on there, and one of the things I like to do that differentiates me is that I put the date and time or something similar on the note. So, that it does not look like a mass-created sticky note. You need something that says that there was an actual person there. Put that or stick it to the house or the door or slip it into the mailbox. Tell them you are interested in purchasing their house and give them a phone number to call. We will get into some of the marketing pieces later on in the book, but if you are going to go driving anyways, you should always have something like that with you.

**It's time to drive around the key areas and streets that you would like to invest in. Be ready with sticky notes.**

- **Keep in mind the housing types that cash flow well in your area – duplexes, freehold townhomes, or semis, whatever you have determined for your area.**

- **Usually, you can narrow down the number of streets that you need to visit by asking a realtor, property manager or fellow investors.**
- **You could also do some research on property purchase prices in the area. So that you understand which areas provide the most opportunity to cash flow.**

Next, I want to give you some actions here; you are going to get off of your computer and take some time after you have identified key areas and streets that you would like to invest in. You should at least bring a sticky notepad with you because you do not have those templates yet and you have not ordered them. Do not make excuses like "I will do it later" or "I will do it next week." Okay, so get out there, and I want you to keep in mind, what types of properties cash flow well in your area. Where are the duplexes? Are they freehold townhouses? Have you determined the area that you are interested in? Usually, you can narrow them down to a number of streets. Be sure to talk to the realtors. Realtors can be great assets for you. If you are a realtor, you have a great opportunity to look through the MLS to find out rent prices and other details.

You can talk to property managers, fellow investors, and use tools like Kijiji.ca or Rentometer.com to find out what are the rents in the area or where people are renting. You can research different property prices. This will help you understand which areas make sense and which areas cash flow. This is an opportunity for you to do some driving. So, stop reading this book, get into your vehicle or get into somebody else's vehicle, and make sure that you start driving around. This is not driving for dollars, but it could be if you just leave a little note and somebody calls you back. This is going to be the first step that will help you become a geographical specialist.

# Chapter 4

# Using Data to Help You Take Action

We are going to go through some terminology that you hear constantly when you are thinking and talking about real estate, particularly in the house flipping space. It is the same thing that we are going to be learning here. Think about it this way...you need to have a point at which you make an offer on the property; I like to call it a "trigger point." A trigger point helps you to know when to take action.

I'm going to explain a few different versions of what investors use to determine when to purchase a property—there is a "trigger point."

The first is called the Maximum Allowable Offer. There are lots of different versions of this, but if you can think about it this way, it is like you are working backwards. So, you take what you are going to sell the property for, subtract the cost of the renovations, add in the holding costs, and a profit margin. This will give you the maximum allowable offer.

Other people have a back-of-the-napkin number that they use. This would be a formula that helps them to determine what to offer on a property. For example they use a 70% Rule, where they add in the purchase price, the cost of renovations, then the selling price and the cost of the renovations, and then they will offer 70% of that to the seller.

Another approach investor's use is the after-repair value of the property, which is what they believe they are going to be able to sell the property for and come up with an offer for a potential seller based on this number, considering the renovation and other costs. Other people will just call this the Max Offer. This is the maximum that I am going to offer you on this property, and they have calculated that in some other way.

However you do it, you need to come up with something that works for you, and I am going to share a few strategies with you that will help you come up with that number, but you are going to have to define the "trigger point" for yourself.

What I would like to suggest that you do is to use a simple spreadsheet. I am going to give you a sample one, and it is up to you whether you decide to use it or not. This one is more of a trigger point on purchasing a buy and hold rental, rather than something for a flip project. I suggest you use something simple. What is the purchase price? Then you want to look at your hard costs, those are costs that are the same month over month. What is the mortgage going to cost you, property taxes, insurance, condo fees if any, rental water tanks, etc.? Then, you will have a trigger point that makes sense for you. Anything that cash flows $200 to $300 is actually decent enough to do a deeper analysis if you are going for a long-term hold, particularly if you are using money partners to help purchase the property. (If this interests you, I suggest you checkout the book, *The Scaling Up Toolbox: A How to Guide for Real Estate Investors Who Don't Have to Use Their Own Money to Buy Property* by Quentin D'Souza.) Furthermore, you are going to have to decide what cash flow number is comfortable for you.

In real estate, there are an infinite number of opportunities to be able to use a spreadsheet. I am going to share this method because it is simple. You can make it as detailed and complex as you want but I would not recommend that. Essentially, what you need to do is have a quick pass filter to see if the property makes sense to purchase.

| | A | B | C | D | E | F | G |
|---|---|---|---|---|---|---|---|
| 1 | **TRIGGER POINT** | | | | | | |
| 2 | **5 Year Fixed Rate** | 3.00% | | **Amortization** | | 30 | |
| 3 | | | | | | | |
| 4 | | **Freeholds** | | **Condos** | | | |
| 5 | **Purchase Price** | 250000 | | 220000 | | | |
| 6 | **Mortgage** | 843 | | 749 | | the mortgage | |
| 7 | **Tax** | 2900 | | 2400 | | payment Is | |
| 8 | **Tax Monthly** | 242 | | 200 | | approximate | |
| 9 | **Insurance** | 45 | | 20 | | | |
| 10 | **Condo Fees** | | | 210 | | | |
| 11 | | | | | | | |
| 12 | **Total** | 1130 | | 1179 | | cash flow before | |
| 13 | **RENT** | 1450 | | 1400 | | maintenance, | |
| 14 | **Profit Before MVR** | 320 | | 221 | | vacancy and repairs | |
| 15 | | | | | | | |
| 16 | | | | | | | |

Next thing you need is to find out what similar properties are selling for in the area or what they might potentially sell for. I am going to share some strategies that will allow you to do that.

What you are going to do is to find some comparables, and if you are a realtor, you can just go search on the MLS backend database and come up with comparables. If you are a real estate agent, I'm going to assume that this is easy enough for you to do. If you are in the US, there are websites like Redfin. com that make the search for comparables so much easier. In Canada, however, it is much more limited because the different real estate associations, particularly in Ontario where some have been fighting to keep this entire data private, but some realtors and brokerages have made this data available through apps as long as you register with them.

Here are some examples and these tools are a great way for you to find different comparables of properties in particular areas. The HouseSigma Ontario Real Estate is a good phone app for finding comparables. You will probably be contacted by a realtor from the company in order to be able to access the service. Zoocasa is a second and the Real Master app is the third one. These are three different apps that you can use to find comparable properties, and access to those tools will change over time; hopefully, there will be many more available in the future with different features. What is pretty simple about these apps is that you put in an address, you look for sold property data in the given area, and you can do it by a map search. There are a few different ways, and you can go back and look at what properties have been sold in the last,60 days, 90 days, 180 days, etc. Really, what you want to look for is comparables from the last 90 days. Sometimes, it is hard to find that because there are just not that many sold properties in an area, and then you cannot find easy comparables. That is where some more advanced appraisal skills such as looking for other types of properties that were sold come in, and in a wider area or price range, and then coming up with an idea of what a price per square foot of a property is, but using apps like those mentioned can be quite helpful for you.

The next thing you can do to find comparable property information would be if you have access to property tax assessment information. Many towns, cities, and areas in the US have their property assessment information available to the public. In Ontario, you will want to try and use the "about my property" tool through

MPAC (mpac.ca). It'll give you a little bit of an understanding of what is happening in an area with regards to prices, an idea of the purchase price, or what the value of that property is. I find that the property assessment is usually a number of years behind what the actual property is but at about the same percentage...if you can find out what that percentage is for a given area.

The best approach for finding comparables, of course, is talking to a realtor, somebody who is very familiar with an area, especially if you have narrowed down your interest to a few neighborhoods. A good realtor is worth their weight in dollar bills because they are familiar with all the recent comps, have a feel for sold prices, and what the potential property would go for. Furthermore, if you can create a good relationship with a realtor, you can make it a win-win situation and you can actually help them to grow their business as well. Let me explain.

If you get a lead and you are not able to do anything with it, you could pass that along to a realtor and have them transact on it. Then, when you need comparables, have them send you the comparables. If you are stuck on something, maybe you can create a relationship this way. There are a lot of realtors that would like to have such an understanding. So, make sure that you keep this in mind.

You will need to understand the comparables for the property that you are interested in, wherever that property lead comes from. If a property comes to you off market and you do not know what it is worth, you are likely going to make a mistake. What I have noticed is that people think they got a super-duper deal because they think that a property is comparable to something other than it really is. And if it is worth $100,000 or more than what they are offering to a potential seller, this will make deals fall through more frequently. Additionally, make sure that you know what the value of the properties is by understanding the comparables in the area.

The other thing is that there are a few more pieces of this puzzle. First, you need to understand what the level of finish is. What is the rental level? Does it have high-end marble countertops? Do we have a steam room? If you are going to carry out any renovations on a property, what level of renovations does it need because that will affect the after-repair value of the property? Really, if you are just doing rental quality, because you are renting out the property afterwards, you may want to make it more presentable.

However, try to avoid over-renovating a property, such as putting granite, oak, and other upgrades into a rental property. It would be better if you are going to sell the property but not necessarily if you are just going to be renting it out. For the long term, you want a level of quality that is going to last for a longer period of time. Consider using vinyl click flooring that lasts for a long time, rather than doing an oak or hardwood flooring, as it is more rental durable and water resistant.

## Renovations

- **Level of Renovation/Finishes Just Above for the Area**
- **Watch for Over-Renovating for a Given Area**
- **Condition Checklist**
- **Geographic Expertise = Level of Finish**

## Strategies if You Have No Clue

- **Bring a Contractor with You**
- **Take Videos and Measurements of All the Areas on Walking Through**
- **Bring an Experienced Investor with You**

What you will also need is to have a "condition checklist." This is a checklist of the different rooms, what they look like, etc. I am going to give you an example of a checklist at www.findingDiscountedProperties.com, but you need to come up with a checklist that works for you. Is the property in a good condition, average condition or does it need work? Those are the pieces that are going to help you, when you start to get out there and make offers on properties because you want to be able to identify what renovations you are going to need to do. If you cannot identify how much it is going to cost, you better figure out strategies to be able to get those numbers because you do not want to make an ill-informed decision.

Similarly, if you have that geographic expertise of an area, you will know if it is a rental area and the level of finishes that you are going to get in that neighborhood. Often, I will do just a little better than what you would see in an area because it gives you the ability to track nicer tenants and rent properties faster, and if you are going to sell a property—sell properties faster. So, having those nicer levels of finishes makes sense, particularly in a flip project, but also, if you are looking at just the level of rental property finish, then you can do without premium finishes.

What if you do not know anything about renovating, which is probably the case for a lot of people. When you get to the point where you are going to visit a property and you have it under contract, that is probably the point where you would bring a contractor in and say, "*Hey, listen, what do you think that it would cost to get this, and this done.*" You can do that at the same time you are getting the inspection of a property done or doing your financing or appraisal, whatever you need to do. You could bring that contractor in at the same time if you are not working with a realtor and you are going directly to the seller. You are bringing somebody with you and you are just letting them know that is what you are doing.

The other thing you can do is take videos, pictures, and measurements of the property so that you can go in and see exactly what the layout of the property is. That will make it easier for you when you plan to do any renovations and you don't have access to the property. You want to be able to share with a realtor or with a contractor what it is that you are doing, or maybe a realtor as well, to get some feedback on the finishes. You can have all those measurements in the videos to help you to do that.

Another way is bringing an experienced investor with you, one who has done a dozen or more similar projects. If you have an experienced investor with you, they can tell you from the levels of finish whether it is a $250,000 home or a million-dollar home. You need to be able to know what it is that you are renovating. That comes with experience and knowing the area that you are in. So, keep that in mind when you are thinking about putting together the offer.

We are first looking at comparables. What is the after-repair value of the property? Then, we are thinking about the renovations that we are going to do to the property and what are the costs. Now, you could spend time developing a spreadsheet, coming up with your own numbers, and trying to identify opportunities. I find that people get so lost in analytics that they never actually do anything. If you are just getting started, which is where I assume that you are, I suggest building good relationships with people that will be able to help you get some ballpark ideas of what renovations will cost, and then during your inspection period, you should be able to identify any problems that come up, if you have an inspection period. Usually, when I am dealing with off market properties, normally I still have inspections. If I am buying it from a wholesaler or off the MLS, I may not have that opportunity, particularly in a competitive market, but in this case, I am finding the property and it is me that is dealing directly with the seller. So, I am going to be able to do things a bit differently.

Let us keep going here. The last bit of information I want to tell you is, again, and I mentioned this before, being a geographic expert helps you to identify the level of finishes in an area, what people are expecting, the benefits of an area. This could mean the difference between you offering $5,000 less for a property, but being able to recapture that, because of the location of the property. Actually, it is more likely that it could be $50,000 because you are a geographic expert. Do you know other things about the area that would make that area more valuable? Remember to keep that geographic expertise there and build that over time. So, again, we want to know exactly what the after-repair value of the property is and what the renovations are going to cost. Then, you would know if you have a bit of a profit margin in there. If it is a flip project, it has to have a decent enough profit margin in there.

So, you have to consider that, and when you do that, you will end up with a trigger point. This is what I can offer for a particular property because it makes sense to me. Then, that would be your maximum allowable offer. That would be your back of the napkin number that you can offer a particular seller, whatever you want to call it. That is what you are going to be giving to a potential seller.

Another little activity here: You are going to spend some time focusing on a few streets in the area for similar sales. Then, you should be coming up with some trigger points for yourself on whether you would buy a property or not. In looking at the comparables, you may not know whether they did any renovations or not to get the price that they did, especially if you don't have access to any pictures.

So, I am going to assume here that there is perhaps 2 percent of the purchase price in closing costs, something really simple like that, as I want you to identify what properties you are going to buy because of the area, the purchase price, and the cash flow. I want you to be certain and develop some confidence around making a good purchase.

You need to decide what area you are going to be buying in. Once you have decided on the area that you are going to be buying in, I want you to decide on that trigger point. What point will you make at the maximum you purchase a property where it makes sense to you because of the rents? If this price is far below what the market will bear, even with renovations then it may be necessary to look at another area. So, what is your trigger point?

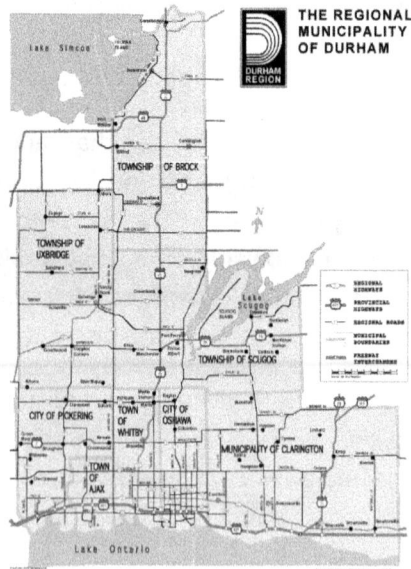

# Chapter 5

# Setting Up a Voicemail System

Now, one of the most important parts of your system is setting up a phone or a voicemail system. There are various options to choose from. We are going to talk through some of them, and we are also going to go through some examples of different ways or systems that are out there. First of all, I want you to recognize how essential this tool is, for not only the lead generation system but the real estate business in general. It helps you prioritize calls that come in. When you have leads, it is great for tracking where the leads come from, you are actually able to see the phone number of the person who called, even if they do not leave a phone number. This makes it easier for you to follow up with them. Furthermore, a lot of the services will offer a voice-to-text feature. This enables you to actually read the information beforehand. I find that it is a really useful tool. Now, there are different options available to choose from, and the tool that I prefer is Grasshopper, which I have been using for over ten years.

So, I know it is a reliable system. Other options include Call Rail, a popular system for real estate investors and wholesalers. It has a CRM (customer relationships management) component, where you can manage calls that come in, assign them to different people, and take notes. So, a lot of people like the Call Rail system, and I suggest giving it a try, as well, to see which one you like. Remember that it is important if you do not like a service, are you able to transport that phone number to another service because it is not always doable. It is something that you want to keep in mind when you are looking over this and the different voicemail systems that are out there.

## Setting up a Voicemail System

- **Essential Tools for Running a Real Estate Business**
- **Prioritize Calls**
- **Track Where Leads Come From**

This is a sample phone script that you can leave on your extension. You can call all the "We Buy Houses" signs that you find and listen to as many messages as you can, to help you to craft your own message. I like to have multiple extensions, and I will explain why, but if you have a pressing need to sell your house, then this is the type of message that will be helpful to you.

## Here is a sample phone script to leave on your extension:

*"If you have a pressing need to sell your house, then this call will be helpful to you. We buy houses—any size, any condition, and any area. We are private investors who buy houses at fair prices. When we buy your house there are no commissions and no fees, just a fast, friendly solution. Most importantly, we can relieve your stress and help you regain your peace of mind. Whether you need instant debt relief, you cannot maintain your house, you are in the midst of bankruptcy, or need cash—we specialize in finding creative solutions to real estate problems others will not touch. You risk nothing when you call to talk to us about selling your house. Please leave your name and number and we will get back to you in the next 48 hours. Thank you."*

I have even seen some investors use two different "We Buy Houses" signs with two different phone numbers on the same street corner or in different areas, but it goes to the same person. This is also an interesting approach, just from a marketing perspective, and adds the idea of competition, I guess. You can utilize different extensions so you can prioritize and track calls, and when calls come in, you want to use a lead buying sheet. I am going to give you an example of one later on in this book. For now, I wanted to just start you off with the voicemail system. So, take some time and explore the different voicemail options that are available in the market.

Remember the key to having voicemail is not to use it at all. If you can pick up the phone and talk to a seller directly it is always better than letting them listen to a recorded message. You are able to make a connection with the seller and perhaps create rapport that will lead you to buying the property. If you do have someone leave a message, make sure to return the call within a few minutes, not hours. The quicker you respond the more likely you are going to get the deal done.

## TIPS:

- **Utilize Different Extensions**
- **Utilize Different Numbers for Different Signs or Areas**
- **Pick Up the Phone**
- **Return Calls Quickly**
- **Phone Existing Signs**
- **Track the Success of Your Ads Using Separate Phone Numbers**

# Chapter 6

# Finding Discounted Properties Takes Time and Money.

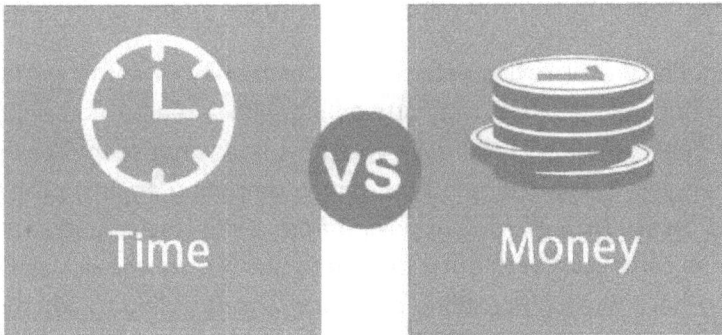

Now, we are looking at the infrastructure that is going to be a part of your system, and I wanted to bring your attention to this concept. It is the primary concept when it comes to lead generation. Especially, when you are starting off as you create and grow a business, you are going to move away from this, but the cost structure is still there. Nonetheless, I am going to address this for new investors and people who are just starting out with lead generation. Think of this as a "bigger picture" concept. Despite what a lot of real estate gurus will tell you, there are two things that you need in order to find homes that run at a discounted rate—it is usually time and/or money. It is a combination of these two things and, usually, you will find that when you are focusing on a person, a real estate asset, a seller, or a specific type of property when you are doing your lead generation. We will go through this in more detail, but I want you to keep in mind, for now, these two things.

Let us say you are looking for a particular person and that person is going to help you find a deal. It is going to take you a lot less time in order to do that, but you are going to have to pay more for that deal. Now, if there is still meat on the bone, there is still an opportunity so you can figure out what makes sense as well as what does not, and you will be able to make money on it.

That first area is saving your time versus money. I want to say that working with a wholesaler or working with a realtor competing on deals on the MLS will save you time. It may not seem like that when you are spending a lot of time competing against properties on the MLS or you are buying from a wholesaler, and sometimes competing with other people to buy from a wholesaler. But they have already identified someone who is willing to sell their property.

Now you are spending less time but you are spending more money because you are paying assignment fees, or you are purchasing the property for a little bit more when competing against other buyers. I am not even including the commissions as part of that just from a realtor, but the fact that you are usually competing against other people, the next area would be finding that motivated seller.

When you are looking for a motivated seller, it will take more time and cost more money. So, when you are in that search, perhaps you are working with advertising, like a flyer campaign, you have to spend the time in order to get that deal done, especially if you are just starting out, and you do not have an assistant to help you in the lead generation capacity. I encourage you not to have an assistant at the beginning because I want you to develop a rapport with sellers, and if you can get a really good rapport, you will be able to get good opportunities.

Having the time to be able to do that is challenging for a lot of people. So, perhaps that is not where you want to spend your time, maybe you are looking for a particular person, you also have to spend money on marketing. People do not realize that some of the wholesalers can spend $15,000 or more a month on advertising in order to get those deals. On social media, like Facebook/Instagram, you just see the person who finishes the marathon but not all the years of work that it took to get up to that point. It is all the years or the months of payments that come up to that wholesaling fee that they charge you. If you are going to do that, you are going to have to spend time and money on marketing in order to find those opportunities.

The next opportunity is a house that nobody wants or knows about. You may have to spend a lot more time trying to figure out what the deal is, by knowing how to solve the problems. Perhaps you run into a situation where the basement has two inches less space to get the height to do a legal basement suite, because of something like vents that are there, or the ducting is lower by two inches. If you are experienced, you may say, "*Well, I can pancake the ducts, do a heat loss test, and make sure that everything is the same, or perhaps I will still be able to do the basement suite,*" whereas somebody else, without that experience and the time that they put into being able to figure that out, wouldn't be able to do that. It may cost you less money because you know how to solve problems that other people cannot, or do not want to deal with, like a hoarder house or a cat pee house—something with hidden potential.

All of those factors are challenges, but if you have the skills to solve those problems, skills that you invested time to learn and developed over time, you will probably spend less money on the house. You will be able to solve those problems that others will not. It is something to keep in mind, both from the advertising and a problem-solving perspective, when it comes to finding discounted properties.

| | Time | Money | Focus |
|---|---|---|---|
| 1. | 🕐 | 💰💰💰💰 | Looking for a Particular Person |
| 2. | 🕐🕐 | 💰💰💰 | Motivated Seller |
| 3. | 🕐🕐🕐 | 💰 | House that Nobody Wants or Knows About |

Now, how can you create a shortcut for this process? Well, if you sign up on wholesalers' mailing lists, then start going out and meeting people, you will get to look at houses. There is no way around it, and if you want to find discounted properties, you need to spend time meeting people who are experts in the area of wholesaling properties. Maybe they are going to earn a commission or an assignment fee from the purchase of the property, but you need to go out and you need to find those people. Those are the people whom you are going to have to pay, but as I said before, enough meat on the bone to make sense and to become an expert in the area.

Being able to solve those problems that other people cannot, is just the way it is, when you have gained experience. If you are going to compete with forty other people on a property that everybody knows about, then you are going to have to pay $20,000 or $200,000, or more. Remember that if you advertise directly in an area and you pull a lead that other people do not know about, or it took you more time than others were willing to do, or you had a little bit of upfront cost, but you got a lot more profit in the deal, you are going to make a lot more money.

## TIP:

TIP: Make sure to **pass on** the deals that do not make sense to you, but make sure to **pass on** the deal to other investors or a realtor. As I have often found that the deals will get passed back to you in the future. The other tip that I want to give you is that whenever you get leads that come in, while you are building your system, make sure that there is a way for you to share leads that you pass on but you are not going to deal with for whatever reason. Maybe another investor can help you. Perhaps they would be willing to take the deal and wholesaler for you, and you get a commission from that or a percentage. You could pass it to a realtor, and you would be creating a good relationship with the realtor, so that in the future you can do some work with them or that they can help give you some comparables, comps, or help you with something else. If you make sure that any lead that you get does not go to waste and make sure that it goes into your system created in a way to ensure that the leads are never wasted.

# Chapter 7

# Leveraging Real Estate Agents (Your Power Team)

When I refer to your Power Team, really, I am referring to real estate agents, mortgage brokers, banks, private lenders, lawyers, appraisers, home inspectors, general contractors, and the people that you work with. For instance, when I am talking about a real estate agent, I still think that agents are one of the best places to go to find an investment property. Preferably, you want a realtor who owns a number of rental properties themselves and has a good grasp of the rental situation in the area that you are investing in. Essentially, you want to find an agent who is a geographic expert.

Any realtor can sell you a property, and they are going to want to sell you a property, but it could be in a bad area of a city or a town, especially if they do not know about it themselves. They should be able to identify streets and housing types, where cash flow makes sense from their investment perspective. A good realtor should be able to listen to what a real estate investor wants, what their goals are, and do their best to meet those goals. Sometimes, investors have certain goals and the realtors present them with something completely different. Being able to leverage the experience of realtors in a specific area, as a Power Team member is crucial to your success.

Oftentimes, I am asked, should I get a real estate license? I say that if you love real estate and you are looking for a job, then I think a realtor is a great place to start. It is also a great way to get experience negotiating and dealing with buyers and sellers. I even recommended that my seventeen-year-old son become a real estate agent when he was old enough. There are a lot of part-time real estate agents that do not make any money, and there are lots of real estate agents in the top 20 percent that generally do. It depends on how you commit your time. I never got my real estate license, nor have I ever wanted to get that license, although I am sure it would have saved me some money selling properties, but it does not really affect my ability to find opportunities, negotiate, or close on opportunities.

Often, I work with realtors very closely, and I know that they can bring me opportunities. They are really willing to work with me because I am not a realtor. This might mean like a fixer-upper property or a quick close situation as I have developed the reputation over time, and I can get those deals done. Perhaps there is a bit of an issue and the seller does not necessarily want to list their property and put a sign online. I am somebody that can step in and help with that situation. I am not competing with the real estate agents, who oftentimes is what they feel that another agent might bring another buyer in, scooping it up from under them.

There are some pros and cons of getting a real estate license. I believe that there are enough opportunities out there and I do not need to get a license to do it. If you are interested in real estate investing and looking to quit your job to start a different career, I think being a realtor is a great place to start. I am not an advocate of becoming a wholesaler to generate income. I think that it is great and it can be quite profitable, but I think it'd be a little bit more challenging. Nineteen out of every twenty wholesalers that I have talked to leave wholesaling within the first few months and the ones that stay, do really well with it. However, they also have something unique about how they are doing things that makes it profitable for them. In a lot of cases, if you are looking for something simple like getting your license, it is an easy way of getting into that transactional side of the business.

If you want to talk to realtors, a great way is just to do an email blast to some of the realtors in the area and then let them follow up with you to see if you are able to create a connection with them. Maybe send them an email, giving them some of your criteria about what you are looking for, so that you are not wasting their time, and they are not wasting yours. If it is something that is not in the criteria, or something that they do not usually focus on, then it is going to be a waste of time, but if you create these relationships and people know who you are, you are more likely to be able to have relationships to get the deals done. The other thing is that you also have to have connections with those people, I know hundreds of realtors but I do not get deals from hundreds of realtors, even though I have a great reputation, but I do get opportunities from some of them, whom I have a relationship with and that are the difference.

So, anybody can do this, it is not just me, as long as you have criteria and they know what you are looking for, and that can be a great opportunity for you. Who do you work with? Sometimes you end up with two realtors who bring you a deal, and I am really upfront with people. I say, "Look, such and such a person brought me this opportunity already and I am working with them." Your reputation will precede you. Some people will stop working with you because you are working with multiple realtors, and that is perfectly fine. Maybe they only have a limited amount of time. If so, then you are not going to have deals with them. They would not want to waste their time with you, and that is completely understandable. You just have to be absolutely clear with the realtor about the property criteria so that you do not lose credibility with them. So, if somebody brings you a deal, it meets your criteria, and you do not put an offer on it, it is going to mean that you are probably not going to get anything from them in the future.

Be careful about how you email blast realtors, as you may get lots of contacts, but you could be wasting a considerable amount of time, especially if they are just pulling listings off the MLS, while you are looking for pocket listings before the signs go up, so that you can put an offer on a small pocket listing. A pocket listing is a potential listing that the realtor has but it is not on the MLS yet. They are shopping around to their contacts and other realtors usually so that they can just get that deal done quickly or for some other reason. Similarly, it could be a listing that is going to go live on the market in a week but the seller has agreed for the listing agent to have an exclusive for seven days. It could allow you to put an offer in with less people having knowledge of the deal. I do have realtors that I have worked with and done straight MLS deals with and they are a part of my original Power Team, but I no longer really work with those realtors in this capacity. I do keep in touch with a lot of realtors, but now I am focused more on the apartment buildings. So, I still have my pulse on what is going on, and if there is an opportunity, I will take advantage of it, but it will have to pass a strict criterion for me to put an offer on the property.

Just remember, you do not want to have multiple realtors presenting the same property off the MLS to you, it will become a real email nightmare for you. Be mindful of that, especially when you are working with realtors who are not sourcing sellers. Sometimes, realtors will work with you when they have a listing that might not be listed on the MLS. Like I said before, if you have an offer, you can put it in there. When they get this done, perhaps they are going to get a commission from the realtor, from the seller, or double end because they are bringing the buyer and they are putting the deal together. So, that can often be a major motivation for the realtor.

However, it is not legal in some provinces. For instance, in BC, if you are reading this, it is not something that you can really take advantage of, but in Ontario, if the realtor can have a double-ended commission and, thus, they are even more motivated to get the deal done with you and their seller. So, that is something to be mindful about with pocket listings and pre-MLS type of opportunities,

Finally, I have been contacted by agents who have trouble selling a property, whatever the reason. So, if I can solve that problem for the agent, they will still get the commission, the property gets sold, and everybody is happy. I am a problem-solver, and I often get calls from agents because they know that I can help them out in such situations. If you develop a rapport as a problem-solver, you will be able to get such opportunities—hoarder houses, quick sales, etc. We have talked a lot about real estate agents but this is true for any of your team members. You always want to make sure that everybody knows that you are buying properties.

You can always offer a lead to a general contractor or lender or people who are actually finding properties that are going to be sold. This is a great opportunity for you to take advantage of and create that infrastructure where you say, *"Listen, if a lead comes in and I buy the property, I am going to give you $1,000."* You can do that as an investor, which is not as easy to do as a real estate agent. Take advantage of doing things this way, because you can sweeten the number of dollars and motivate them even more, and that way you can get a deal done.

# Chapter 8

# The Multiple Listing Service (MLS)

While I have said that the off market is remarkable, the MLS is still interesting for opportunities, and I will explain why. This is probably more about the discounted properties rather than the off market properties, but it is important not to overlook using MLS, as this is where everybody goes to list their properties. That does not mean that you should not use it, it just means you have to be wary. You need to keep track of what is coming in on the market. Even though, like in a hot market, you should be trying to get listings every day to see what is on there and what is coming in, and ask a realtor to send you a daily MLS blast of properties that meet your criteria in a given area.

Maybe they are houses under $600K in a specific area, perhaps it is properties with one or two kitchens or something similar in the area. Whatever is the criteria that you are tracking, you want to make sure that you are finding out what is going on in the area and keeping up to date. The reason is simple, you cannot make offers on things where your mind is stuck at a five-year-old price, as opposed to the current price. You cannot be buying a detached house in Oshawa for $260K because that is what you thought it went for five years ago, it simply is not going to work. You need to be aware of what the properties and their values are so that you can make an offer and then get a discount, and get the deal done.

**53 Little Ave, Clarington**
$399,900 · NEW · MLS# E5157845
4 bed · 2 washroom · Semi-Detached, Backsplit 4

**50 Hartsfield Dr, Clarington**
$589,900 · NEW · MLS# E5158209
3 bed · 2 washroom · Semi-Detached, Bungalow-I

**71 Staples Ave, Clarington**
$598,990 · NEW · MLS# E5156742
3 bed · 2 washroom · Detached, 2-Storey

**27 Soper Creek Dr, Clarington**
$599,900 · NEW · MLS# E5157037
3 bed · 2 washroom · Detached, 2-Storey

View Details

This is a simple example of daily listings or a blast of listings. Oftentimes, when you get a listing, you really want to be aware of what is going to make sense to purchase or not. Here is an example of a listing that was sent recently. The listing price is $399,900 and it is a semi-detached house in Bowmanville. It has a finished basement with a separate entrance. Notice that it has a baseboard, electric heat, not forced air, and it has a large above-grade window—all of these things are telling me this is a good opportunity with three parking spots.

We know that in Bowmanville, or if you didn't know, you can actually do three parking spots back-to-back, one in front of the other. In Oshawa, you need to have at least two parking spots that are accessible at all times. So, knowing the municipality helped me identify this as a great opportunity. I know the area as well because I had an appraisal done on the street. I know this and I can look at some of the comps that we have been looking at before. We saw that in the first section of the book. I know that this property is listed at a much lower price than what it is going to sell for and would have multiple offers. So, all of those things are in here, and you will see that in the listing too.

There is a virtual tour so I can actually have a better look inside, but right off the bat, I know that this house is probably a great candidate for basement suite conversion, so let us think this through a little more. Say we go on and we see the details of the listing. There is some information on who is selling the property. Often, this is found on the realtor side of things but you can see that here. Often, you find out who is selling. Whether it is in the estate of somebody or a lender. I have even purchased properties from accidental owners—whatever it is, it'll affect your ability or they will affect how you put an offer in on a property. They would be looking at just the best offer or closing the property quickly and getting it off their books. Whatever that is, you should be able to look at the listing and find out the details about who is selling the property, as it will affect how you approach the property.

Look for the keywords in the descriptions, such as handyman special, needs work, perfect for investor, needs TLC, as is, where is, motivated seller, undervalue. You want to be able to look at these keywords and, perhaps, you can get your realtor to add this to their search criteria for you, or they could have other criteria that will be helpful for you to use. The key here is to find properties as quickly as you can, and get in there, figure out whether or not to make an offer, and every little bit helps. These description keywords are helpful for me.

## Description Keywords:

"Handyman Special," "Needs Work," "Perfect for Investor," "Needs TLC," "As Is," "Where Is," "Motivated Seller," or "Undervalue."

Another thing that I look for in properties, which is a little different, is to look for whether it has been on the market for a long time.

Now, in a very heated competitive market, it does not happen very often, but these are usually properties that nobody wants for some reason. I bought a property that I had to put money into. It was out on Grandview in Oshawa, and I bought it off the MLS. It had been on the MLS for over sixty days. There were holes in the roof, water coming down, cat pee smell everywhere, and there was actually a mask that the realtor had left on the countertop to wear as you walk through the house. Those are the properties that have been on the market for a long time and have some issues. They can be a great opportunity for you to take advantage of, especially if you know how to solve problems. We keep going back to the problem-solving ability, and it takes time to master that art.

Sometimes you will have sellers that are relisting properties. They have closed their listing, relist it again, they could be very motivated. You can have a realtor send you those properties that have been on the market for a long time. If you can figure out how to solve the problem, or whatever the issue is, in order to bring the property to its highest and best use, still make money and cash flow on the property, then you are golden. Especially if it is a property that has been there for a long time. We are going to talk briefly about foreclosures in Canada. Often, in Canada, homes that are being foreclosed on, there are two ways that they go through the process. The first way is through an auction sale at a courthouse where you have multiple bidders. Usually, this is a mortgage company that will buy out any property that is below the mortgage balance.

If you are bidding on a property in the courthouse, you will not have time to do additional due diligence on the property and you will not get a chance to get any inspections done. You will have the ability to purchase the property outright. Usually, this is like a tax sale type of situation more than anything, and then oftentimes I find that these properties are being bought back by the seller or at the least the person who has to sell the property at the last minute. The second way, which is mostly in Ontario, as other provinces are different, but it is through the MLS through a realtor. If a house is listed on the MLS, you can identify who is selling it and whether it is a bank.

The realtors usually have a good relationship with the different financial institutions and seem to get a funnel for these properties. Sometimes, institutions will try to spread out a bit. It is important to have good relationships and a good reputation for closing, but do not expect them to do you any favors. There is always some value to a realtor, particularly if there is a double commission, but I think that the seller would be suspicious if they were always double ending the commission. This is also something to be mindful of, when and why building relationships is crucial. Please understand that the MLS is still a great place to build some infrastructure for your lead generation business.

# Build Relationships

Listed for over 90 days

Particular problems that most investors might find difficult to solve

Pets have urinated and/or defecated

Heavy smokers

Problem tenant.

I want to reiterate that building relationships is the key when you are doing a walkthrough of a property from the MLS, to be keen on properties that are vacant or have been listed for over ninety days, have some price reduction which indicates that the seller is probably motivated to sell the property. Furthermore, look for particular problems with properties that investors or homeowners might find difficult to solve and create a system to eliminate those problems, such as pet odors. Well, perhaps one of the things that you are going to do is take that right down to the subfloor, remove all the carpeting, all the flooring, seal the flooring, etc.

Before you do that, maybe you clean it with some bleach or with a different combination of chemicals, and then you seal it with a kilns-based product, use an ozone machine—have whatever system that can help you eliminate that odor. You will be able to solve a problem that somebody else will not undertake those relationships that you have built with the realtors and your problem-solving reputation means that the next time such a property comes up, they will be approaching you. This means that you will not have to do the work to generate it, by doing the work of building relationships with those particular realtors.

# Chapter 9

# For Sale by Owner

Now, there are quite a few "for sale by owner" websites on the internet. You are going to find this kind of funny but the more obscure the "for sale by owner" website you see a listing on, the more likely you are going to find a motivated seller, as they are even aware of the more popular "for sale by owner" websites. From my experience, the longer they have been posted on the sites, though, the less likely you are going to get a deal with them, as they probably sold the property, left the listing up, or just are really interested in selling.

- http://www.forsalebyowner.ca
- http://www.forsalebyownercanada.com
- http://www.housemaxx.ca/
- http://www.canada4salebyowner.com

I do not find using the sites particularly useful. I will occasionally have a look at them but they change from time to time. I would say that some sites are better than others but there are a couple of key points here. Here are some examples of places that you can go to find lists of properties for sale. Some of these sites allow you to get email alerts of new listings when they become available. It would be a great idea to sign up for these alerts so that you can keep track of what is going on. So, we have House Max, Kijiji, Craigslist, etc. Again, these are sources for private listings. There are a couple of bigger "for sale by owner" websites that tie into the MLS system. Property Guys, Listed by Seller, One Percent Realty, Purple Bricks—you should definitely sign up for alerts on these sites, but on occasion, I find properties that are posted on these sites first before they move them on to the MLS system, which is quite interesting.

In most cases, you will find that on these sites, people who are trying to sell the house are trying to keep as much money as possible, and as a real estate investor, I have not really found much success in finding motivated sellers from here. What I usually find are people who want way too much for properties and are not willing to give enough to even pay a realtor to make the purchase worthwhile. Most seem to sit on the market for months before they finally sell. Some, after price reductions, are moved to the MLS.

- https://propertyguys.com/
- https://services.listedbyseller.ca/
- https://ontario.onepercentrealty.com
- https://purplebricks.ca

The other thing that you can do is just keep your eye out for such signs. I look for signs all the time for open houses, signs for people who are selling privately or for sale by owner houses.

Oftentimes, the signs are on the window or in the lawn. You can look for different types of signs like coming soon, particularly for the Property Guys or any of those low-cost sites, as it is an easy way to do a door knock and see if any opportunities come around. Just be on the lookout for them and talk directly with the sellers. It is your advantage as a real estate investor, particularly when you

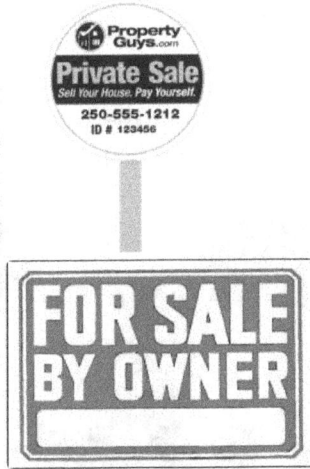

are doing a deal. Usually, you have a realtor who is in between, and it is almost like a broken telephone, you may or may not get all the details that you need to make a deal happen or to find the proper motivation. There is a difference between a realtor sign and then a "for sale by owner" sign.

When I am driving around, I always try to drive down new roads and streets to see if there are any "for sale" signs that I didn't know about or "coming soon" signs for realtors that I can pre-call to inquire about the possible opportunity and what the deal is going to be before it actually gets listed.

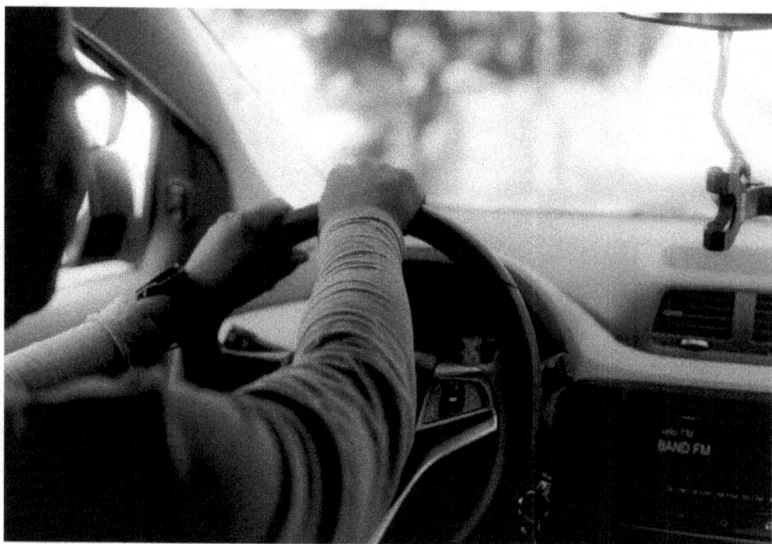

I look for signs that have been stuck on the lawn for a long time— old or faded. It could mean that the person tried to sell their property, but they couldn't, and maybe there was something that was holding them back from selling it. It could be the condition of the property or it could be something else, so I see this as an opportunity. Some people call this Driving for Dollars, as part of the infrastructure of your business, you want to keep driving down different roads and see if any opportunities come up.

Another thing that I also look for are "Garage Sale Signs." I know this is kind of counterintuitive but a lot of people will do a garage sale before they sell a house. You can always ask at a garage sale. Something like, *"You are doing the sale here, are you thinking about selling your house?"* If so, then you could always get some details on whether they are selling the property or not. There are many ways and places for you to find such opportunities. You have to have an idea of where the person is going to sell their property. If you can come up with some ideas and you create infrastructure around that, you can generate leads for yourself.

# Chapter 10

# Private Sales

- **Private sales fall under the category of "nobody knows about them."**
- **If you are going to go down the path of doing private sales, you need to get a good real estate lawyer on your side and have them help you through the purchase process and avoid mistakes.**
- **Pay a realtor.**

Private sales fall under the category of "nobody knows about them." The second property that I ever purchased as an investor was a private sale. We actually wrote down the terms of the purchase on the back of a napkin and both signed it. We had a real estate lawyer draw up the purchase agreement, and I bought the property. I would say that 75 percent of all the purchases that I have done have been private sales or off market or pocket listings, and they have offered me the best opportunity for discounts as there are fewer people who know about the property that is available for sale. If you are going down this path, you need a good real estate lawyer on your team.

However it is, you want to have help to go through the process and avoid purchasing mistakes. A real estate lawyer can help you with the legal components of the deal. Similarly, they will make sure that you go through the agreement, or you just pay a realtor. Some realtors, if you offer them a commission, we will help you go through the process as well.

- **Get some experience by doing traditional MLS deals with a realtor first before you go down the path of private sales.**
- **If you have these deals, then you can use your purchase agreement as a template.**
- **You can find typical clauses in the Schedule A of a purchase agreement for a private sale.**

You need to get some experience with doing traditional MLS deals with a realtor first before you go down the path of private sales. It could be a personal residence or your first investment property but go through the regular process first. You do not know what it is going to be like unless you have done it. When you have those deals under your belt, you will also have a purchase and sale agreement template that you can use.

Full disclosure, I am not a lawyer, I am not a paralegal, and you will need to get the proper advice. You will be able to find typical clauses in the schedule of a purchase and sale agreement, and then you could use those for a private sale. There are some typical ones for instance:

> "This offer is conditional upon the buyer arranging at the buyer's own expense, a new mortgage satisfactory to the buyers in the buyer sole and absolute discretion, unless the buyer is given notice in writing delivered to the seller within six business days or banking days after the acceptance of this offer, provided that this condition is fulfilled. However, this offer shall be null and

*void, and the deposit shall be returned to the buyer in full. Without the deduction, this condition is included for the benefit of the buyers and may be waived at the sole the, buyer sole option in writing to the seller within the time period stated herein."*

So, what this says is that within six days, you need to actually send a waiver saying that this condition has been fulfilled. If it hasn't, then you are backing out on your offer and you have not fulfilled that condition. It is possible that you can save the offer but there would be a few steps that you would need to do to ensure that it happens. It is something that you want to discuss with your lawyer.

Here is another example of a typical clause that you would use for a home inspection. The previous example was for financing. This one is for home inspection:

*"This offer is conditional upon the buyer obtaining at his or her expense an inspection of the subject property by a registered home inspector within six business days, excluding Saturday, Sunday, or a holiday of acceptance of this offer. In the event such an inspection reveals deficiencies in the subject property, which the buyer is unwilling to accept, the offer shall be null and void and the deposit returned in full without deduction. The seller agrees to cooperate in providing access to the property for the purpose of this inspection. This condition is included for the benefit of the buyer and may be waived at his or her sole discretion by notice in writing to the seller within the time period stated."*

Again, this is a waiver type of position where you need to make sure that this is done within six business days because if it is not done, then it is assumed null and void. Provided that the process has ended and you are no longer buying the property, again, this is something to be mindful of and done properly. Make sure you have a lawyer to guide you through this part of the process if it is your first time.

One of the clauses that I often include is subject to lawyer review of the agreement of purchase and sale contract. One of the things that you may do is have them feel confident, let them review, you could say that for the seller and buyer to review, but whatever it is, give an option in the contract with either party to get out of the contract if the lawyer says that the agreement of purchase and sale is not something that makes sense, for whatever reason.

One of the other clauses that I include is the option, *"This offer is subject to the seller's property not currently being represented by an agent or realtor."* The reason why I include this clause is because I do not want to get the surprise of having to pay a commission, just in case that they have enlisted the help of a realtor to sell their property but didn't inform the realtor that they are selling it privately. We want to avoid such situations.

You need to have a lawyer go through this process with you. Go through the clauses if you need some help with them. There are purchase agreement templates and nonstandard agreement templates. You can build customized purchase agreements with clauses and have them readily accessible for use. You can cut and paste clauses out from previous agreements from your realtor or your real estate agent and use them in your agreement. If you have already done that, and you have gone to transactions, the wording is already there to use. Typically, you can find quite unique opportunities with private sales. If you are not using the standard provincial forms and use a nonstandard agreement, it could be quite challenging to work with another lawyer because they have to review the whole contract and they may not want to do that. So, they may actually, if you give them a nonstandard purchase and sale agreement, just ask you to put it on the standard form what they have used in the past and which they are familiar with.

You need to be prepared to know how to deal with different institutions. Let us say it is the lawyers, for instance, or if it is a lending institution, when you are dealing with a property in a private sale. Sometimes, if a person is behind a few months on their rent or mortgage and wants to sell their property, we need to make sure that we can handle it and close the property quickly. So, we want to make sure that in our agreement, we cover the ability to close on that property, from an agreement perspective, as part of your background infrastructure. Typically the Ontario Real Estate Association has standard Purchase and Sale agreement forms, and then there are nonstandard forms. Let us go through them, they both have a similar outline.

You can see here that this is an agreement for purchase and sale. I have my name on it, and you put the seller's name in there with their address. Along with that, if you have any dimensions of the property, what side it is, what city is the property located in, and what is the frontage depth of the lot. There, you are going to put the amount of the purchase and then put it in words. Then, you can see that the deposit is laid out here, how much it is, and who it is going to be paid to—sellers, a lawyer in trust, or me.

So, whoever the seller's lawyer is, you will give them the check in trust so that the transaction is closed. Then, how you are going to do it, upon acceptance, and defining what that is within forty-eight hours. When you and the buyer have both accepted the deal, then you are going to get that deposit over to the seller's lawyer and you are going to write it in trust. You can see the articles that

# Agreement of Purchase and Sale

This Agreement of Purchase and Sale dated this ................ day of ............................. 2009;

**BUYER,** Quentin D'Souza and/or assigns, agrees to purchase from **SELLER,**
............................., .................................................... the following **REAL PROPERTY:**

Address: ..................................................................................... fronting on the
...................... side of ........................................in the City of .............................
and having a frontage of ............. feet more or less by a depth of .................. feet more or
less and legally described as a family dwelling (the "property").

**PURCHASE PRICE:**            Dollars (CDN$) .................................................................
................................................................................................................ Dollars (CDN$)

**DEPOSIT:** Buyer submits Upon Acceptance and fulfillment of terms as listed in Schedule A
attached One Thousand and One Dollars (CDN$) 1001.00 by negotiable cheque payable to
Sellers Lawyer "Deposit Holder" to be held in trust without interest pending completion or other
termination of this Agreement and to be credited toward the Purchase Price on completion.

For the purposes of this Agreement, "Upon Acceptance" shall mean that the Buyer is required to
deliver the deposit to the Deposit Holder within 48 hours of the acceptance and fulfillment of
terms as listed in Schedule A attached of this Agreement. Buyer agrees to pay the balance as
specifically set out in Schedule A attached.

**SCHEDULE(S) A** attached hereto form(s) part of this Agreement.
**1. CHATTELS INCLUDED:**
* Fridge, Stove, Washer, Dryer, Dishwasher, Window Coverings, All Chattels

**2. FIXTURES EXCLUDED:**

**3. RENTAL ITEMS:** The following equipment is rented and **not** included in the Purchase Price.
The Buyer agrees to assume the rental contract(s), if assumable:
* Hot Water Heater

**4. IRREVOCABILITY:** This Offer shall be irrevocable by Buyer until 6:00 pm three (3) business
days from the date of this agreement, after which time, if not accepted, this Offer shall be null
and void and any deposits shall be returned to the Buyer in full without interest;

**5. COMPLETION DATE:** This Agreement shall be completed by no later than 6:00 p.m. on
the......................day of..................................., 2009, Upon completion, vacant possession of
the property shall be given to the Buyer unless otherwise provided for in this Agreement;

**6. NOTICES:** The Buyer states he is not an Agent, Realtor™, or broker;

**7. GST:** If this transaction is subject to Goods and Services Tax (G.S.T.), then such tax shall be
included in the Purchase Price. If this transaction is not subject to G.S.T., Seller agrees to certify
on or before closing, that the transaction is not subject to G.S.T;

This form must be initialed by all parties to the Agreement of Purchase and Sale.

INITIALS OF BUYER(S):                          INITIALS OF SELLER(S):

are included in the agreement. So, in this agreement, the fridge, stove, washer, dryer, dishwasher, etc. You want to make sure that if there are things that you do not want them to take away, it is mentioned in the agreement, any rental items, such as hot water heaters, as well as the revocable period, how many days it takes before the unaccepted offer goes dead, and it is no longer valid.

So, you want to mention that date, along with the completion date, when the actual offer is going to be completed, and you are actually going to close on the property in the future.

Next, there is a title search. When is the title search allowed? How long is it allowed for? Here is the tip: For purchase and sale agreement, again, some typical clauses here for the purchase and sale agreement, it is not my intention to replace your lawyer. You need to go through a lawyer to review these documents if you need to. Understand each term individually, but these are all outlined in the purchase and sale agreement—standard terms, time limits, and how different components are dealt with. You are going to sign it as a buyer, and have it witnessed and dated. Then, the same thing is going to happen for the seller, so the seller is going to sign it and date it.

If for example, the seller has a spouse or the spouse of the buyer that needs to be part of it—one who is on the title for this particular property. For instance, if the seller is selling the property, the seller is on the title, but they have a spouse, then this spouse would sign in as a witness and date it. Sometimes, this is challenging, particularly in a divorce situation, when you are going back and forth between one spouse and the other. It can be quite a challenge, and then confirmation is the date it gets accepted and who accepted it. In this case, it would be the seller or the buyer. If the seller has finally accepted it and the buyer have signed, everything is done. The seller has the final acceptance, then they will sign this, sometimes it is the buyer that has the final

8. **TITLE SEARCH:** Buyer shall be allowed until 6:00 p.m. twenty (20) business days from the date of this agreement, (Requisition Date) to examine the title to the property and until the earlier of: (i) thirty days from the later of the Requisition Date or the date on which the conditions in this Agreement are fulfilled or otherwise waived or; (ii) five days prior to completion, to satisfy himself that there are no outstanding work orders or deficiency notices affecting the property, that its present use as a family dwelling (owner occupied and/or rented and/or leased) may be lawfully continued and that the principal building may be insured against risk of fire. Seller hereby consents to the municipality or other governmental agencies releasing to Buyer details of all outstanding work orders affecting the property, and Seller agrees to execute and deliver such further authorizations in this regard as Buyer may reasonably require during Buyers due diligence;

9. **FUTURE USE:** Seller and Buyer agree that there is no representation or warranty of any kind that the future intended use of the property by Buyer is or will be lawful except as may be specifically provided for in this Agreement;

10. **TITLE:** Provided that the title to the property is good and free from all registered restrictions, charges, liens, and encumbrances except as otherwise specifically provided in this Agreement and save and except for (a) any registered restrictions or covenants that run with the land providing that such are complied with; (b) any registered municipal agreements and registered agreements with publicly regulated utilities providing such have been complied with, or security has been posted to ensure compliance and completion, as evidenced by a letter from the relevant municipality or regulated utility; (c) any minor easements for the supply of domestic utility or telephone services to the property or adjacent properties; and (d) any easements for drainage, storm or sanitary sewers, public utility lines, telephone lines, cable television lines or other services which do not materially affect the present use of the property. If within the specified times referred to in paragraph 8 any valid objection to title or to any outstanding work order or deficiency notice, or to the fact the said present use may not lawfully be continued, or that the principal building may not be insured against risk of fire is made in writing to Seller and which Seller is unable or unwilling to remove, remedy or satisfy or obtain insurance save and except against risk of fire in favor of the Buyer and any mortgagee, (with all related costs at the expense of the Seller), and which Buyer will not waive, this Agreement not withstanding any intermediate acts or negotiations in respect of such objections, shall be at an end and all monies paid shall be returned without interest or deduction and Seller, Listing Brokerage and Co-operating Brokerage shall not be liable for any costs or damages. Save as to any valid objection so made by such day and except for any objection going to the root of the title, Buyer shall be conclusively deemed to have accepted Seller's title to the property;

11. **CLOSING ARRANGEMENTS:** Where each of the Seller and Buyer retain a lawyer to complete the Agreement of Purchase and Sale of the Property, and where the transaction will be completed by electronic registration pursuant to Part III of the Land Registration Reform Act, R.S.O. 1990, Chapter L4 and the Electronic Registration Act, S.O. 1991, Chapter 44, and any amendments thereto, the Seller and Buyer acknowledge and agree that the exchange of closing funds, non-registrable documents and other items (the "Requisite Deliveries") and the release thereof to the Seller and Buyer will (a) not occur at the same time as the registration of the transfer/deed (and any other documents intended to be registered in connection with the completion of this transaction) and (b) be subject to conditions whereby the lawyer(s) receiving any of the Requisite Deliveries will be required to hold same in trust and not release same except in accordance with the terms of a document registration agreement between the said lawyers. The Seller and Buyer irrevocably instruct the said lawyers to be bound by the document registration agreement which is recommended from time to time by the Law Society of Upper

This form must be initialed by all parties to the Agreement of Purchase and Sale.

INITIALS OF BUYER(S):                          INITIALS OF SELLER(S):

acceptance, and the cross-off seller can put in the word "buyer" and then sign it. Then, your private sale agreement is complete.

This is Schedule A, where you have different agreements that we have talked about before. You see that there is some variation here, around subject to an inspection of the sale of the property.

## Schedule A
**Agreement of Purchase and Sale**

This Schedule is attached to and forms part of the Agreement of Purchase and Sale between:

**BUYER,** Aaron Moore and/or assigns, and **SELLER,** ...........................................
......................................................... for the purchase and sale of
................................................... in the City of ...................................................... dated
the .................. day of ................................., 2009.

Buyer agrees to pay the balance as follows:

1. This offer is subject to and contingent upon the inspection of said property by Buyer's investors within 16 business days of acceptance of this offer. Should Buyers Investors not approve of said property the Sellers do hereby advise, authorize and instructs the attorney to immediately refund all earnest money deposits back to the Buyer;

2. The Buyer has the right to assign the agreement of purchase and sale to a 3rd party on or before the closing date;

3. Subject to lawyer review of 'Agreement of Purchase and Sale' contract;

4. Subject to the Seller having given full disclosure at the time of Buyers due diligence;

5. This offer is subject to the Sellers property NOT currently being represented by a licensed Agent, Realtor™, or broker.

This form must be initialed by all parties to the Agreement of Purchase and Sale

INITIALS OF BUYER(S):          INITIALS OF SELLER(S):

In this case, we put sixteen business days, and I want to highlight some of the different things that you can do as a private seller that you might not normally do when you are working with a realtor. They will have certain conditions or things that they have done all the time. Whereas you can do things a little bit differently? There is the opportunity to be different and have a different approach because you have the flexibility to deal directly with the seller. Now, the last bit of advice and it is related more to the infrastructure. I want to remind you that you want to advertise as much as possible.

## Advertise. Advertise. Advertise.

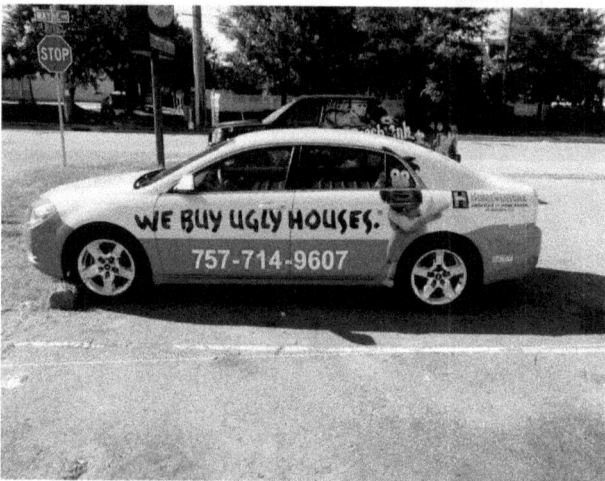

We will go through advertising in more detail in the next chapter, but I want to remind you, again and again, there are different ways to advertise—flyers, stickers, tear sheets at grocery stores, sandwich board signs, bandit signs, business cards, door hangers, online websites, etc. You just need to look and see who can purchase a property so that they could call you and make a connection. You want to make sure that you are present there. You need to create a funnel of deals that are constantly coming your way and it is your job to sift through the opportunities.

I have heard of interesting stories, where someone had a sibling or perhaps a child that wanted to get their driver's license and ultimately a car. They could tell them, "Hey, I will buy you the car but I need you to drive it with a sign on it." Maybe that is a little going too far but you get the idea. You just want to get out there and keep marketing because that is how you fill your funnel and get leads coming in. We will get deeper into the marketing later in the book.

# Chapter 11

# Focusing on a Specific Area

## Focusing on a specific area

- **Farm the area.**

- **Once you have narrowed down the geographic area, you should start to see a pattern emerge where specific areas and specific streets have lots of specific types of investment property that you want to purchase.**

Instead of trying to do a broad-based approach, we want to focus on what I often call "farming the area." Once you have narrowed down your geographic area, you should start to see a pattern emerge where specific areas and streets have a lot of investor properties. Those investor properties are the ones that you are interested in. If you can focus on those areas and focus your marketing, you are more likely to be able to generate a potential lead that can give you an off market deal.

So, how can you do this? Well, firstly, you want to talk to other investors, find out where they are investing, and build a list of the streets and areas where you want to focus. Take some time to list out any streets that keep coming up when you are looking for cash-flowing rental properties.

When you go to investor gatherings or networking events, ask people where they have their rental properties. Take a note of that area. Are there areas that you want to avoid, particularly in a town or a general area? Are there streets that realtors recommend or suggest as good places to find rental properties? Usually, there are a few areas, for instance, that have a lot of semi-detached houses that have accessory apartments or that can easily be converted. In general, it is a four- or five-block radius where you find lots of rental properties that make sense and that can be converted easily. Maybe these are single-family home rentals or multifamily buildings that make sense in a given area. Wherever it is that you want to focus, build that list of streets in areas to focus on because once you do that, then we can start building some marketing campaigns.

- **Build a list of areas / streets that you are interested in focusing on.**
- **Take a few minutes and list out any streets that keep coming up when you are looking for cash flowing rental properties.**
- **Where are other investors buying property?**
- **What streets do realtors suggest as a good place to find rental property?**

Once you have identified the streets that work, you are going to stop waiting for a deal to appear. Stop looking at the MLS for a deal to magically emerge in those areas. It will help though, when you see something that comes up because you can pursue the deal as you know it makes sense. The idea is to separate yourself from what everybody else is doing—and everybody else is going to be looking at the MLS. So, if you solely base your ability to purchase on the MLS, you are going to compete with everybody else, or you can do something different that nobody else or a few investors are willing to do in that area.

I have spent thousands of dollars taking creative real estate investing courses and tried a variety of techniques - in particular the "yellow letter" marketing campaign. Here is a sample of what the yellow letter marketing looks like:

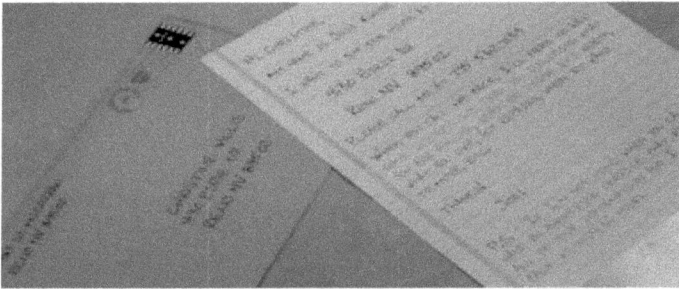

Using a yellow letter helps it stand out. It is different, and you want to make the letter look like it is actually handwritten by a real person. Often, people will have a yellow letter background or orange letter background and they use handwriting or printing type, and that way they are able to print many of them. The main idea is to have a handwritten envelope because that way it looks like a personal letter, and it is more likely to be opened as opposed to an automated letter. That is the real key—to get it opened. Whatever your marketing pieces are, you want them to be opened, and not thrown out as soon as they see the typeface on the letter. Then, once you have them open it and they see the yellow, they would want to read it.

What do you put in that letter? Well, here are a couple of examples of what I have seen in the past:

> Hi, my name is Alex and I am interested in buying properties in your area. I am <u>not</u> a real estate agent.
>
> $$ I BUY HOUSES IN CASH $$
>
> If you have considered selling for any reason
>
> CALL ANYTIME, I WILL RESPOND FAST
>
> What I offer:
> - Fair cash offer, I pay closing costs, no additional fees
> - As-is condition, no need to clean, repair, deal with home inspectors or agents
> - I can close when YOU choose, with the lawyer of YOUR choice
> - No obligations, headaches, or showings, other than my visit
>
> Thank you for your consideration.
> Respectfully,
>
> PS: Keep this letter in a safe place, even if you do not want to sell. If you hear about someone who does, I will pay you at least $500 or more if I buy that property,
>
> NO QUESTIONS ASKED!

There are different ways to go about this, but the way that I like to do it is to say, *"Look, I am somebody who is going to be able to close quickly on this property. I do not care about the condition of the property. I can let you choose the closing. We will not do showings,"* which may be a concern, but whatever it is, we want to make sure that we make it a win-win situation for them. Despite what some people will tell you, not everybody is concerned about getting the highest price. Sometimes, there are other factors that are in play that make more sense for people. You want to approach those people and give them options, and that is what you are going to achieve with this type of letter campaign.

Here is another example of a letter campaign. You will notice that these all look handwritten but all are printed. They appear like they were written by hand, and the dollar signs are even a bit darker than what you would normally see on a handwritten letter.

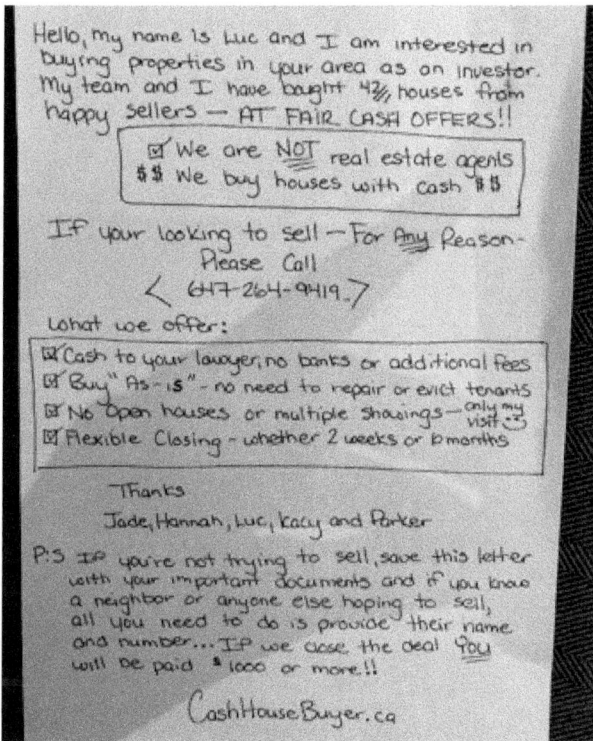

Again, you can do this in different ways, but these are all printed, they are not all handwritten. The interesting thing about this one is that there are multiple people that are listed in this particular letter. They have boxed out what they are offering to add, and this helps it stand out. There is also a local phone number. You will notice that wherever they are advertising, there is probably a local phone number, versus a 1-800 number. These minor details can make a big difference when you want somebody to follow up with you. They have also added a website so people can check their previous buys, testimonials, etc. Essentially, they are trying to make it easier for people to do their own research about them and then reach out once they are ready to sell.

Here is another similar letter, a different version but a bit more concise.

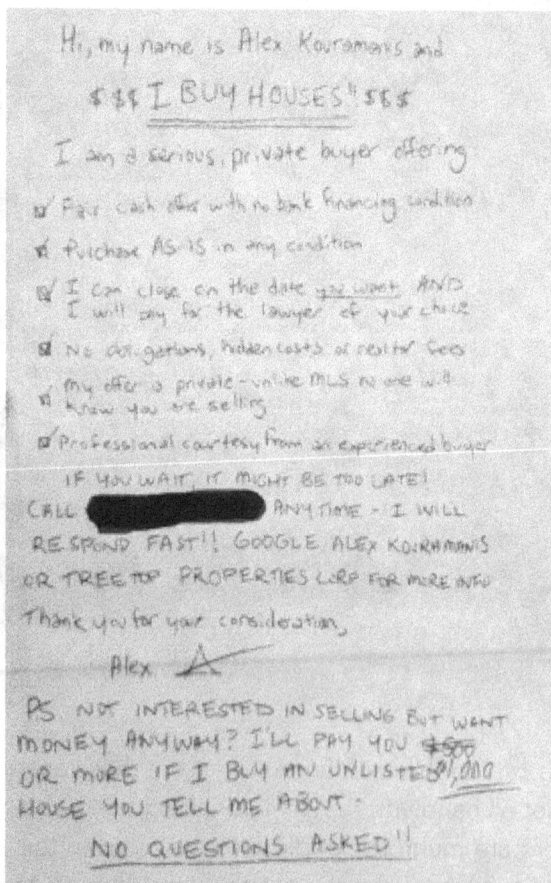

It mentions a referral, which is an interesting addition. If you know somebody else who is selling and you can connect me, I will give you a referral fee. It makes you think, *"Oh, it was $500 but now I am gonna give you $1,000."* If you started off with just putting $1,000 on there, it would be very different than scratching out $500 and putting $1,000 like the old there are even, *"I am going to give you even more than what somebody else might."* There are some well thought out marketing pieces that are going out, whether you think about it or not. Anytime you see these marketing pieces, you should always collect them. That is what I do. It helps you to be a little bit critical about it, to think and ask questions, like why did they do that? Why did they underline certain things? Why did they have boxes with check marks beside them? Why did they have a signature? You should be collecting these and then you can use them as part of your marketing.

A few things that you will need are the names and addresses of people to send these handwritten letters to. You can find these lists by ordering them online. There are several list sources. You could hire a virtual assistant to help you to develop using the 411.ca or online services and to collect as many names and addresses of people as you can for a given area. You can buy that information from different companies. For instance, there is Geowarehouse or there are other listing services where you can buy names. It depends on how much you want to spend to put this list together.

Yellow letter campaigns are very popular in the US, but it is a little different in Canada. Canadians are not used to the same marketing approach, so you may have to cast your net over a wider region to get leads. You can also do multiple campaigns, especially if you are in an area where many people are running similar campaigns, it may not be as effective. It is an interesting way to generate leads, but you have to find out what is working in a given area. Depending on the amount of work that is required and the number of leads that are generated, this may not be the approach for you, but the only way to figure that out is to test it out, especially over a few months. You cannot just do something like this once and think that you are going to get leads.

Sometimes you will have to do the first mail out, then in three months, then in nine months, then maybe month eighteen to gauge whether this is working for you or not. I know that there have been some modifications to this type of technique. You can find opportunities like when someone is about to list a property and you can buy it before they list it. Perhaps you are not getting the same sort of discount but you are able to buy it without the competition. Maybe they pay a percentage of realtor fees on the transaction or it could be 10 percent below the market price. Whatever it is, any of those things could be good enough for you, especially if it is in an area where there is cash flow, and it makes sense to invest in a marketing campaign like this but remember to keep track of it.

When you start working in this manner, you start to develop an area of expertise. Which streets make sense and which ones do not? You should always have all your financing in place, who is going to be the property manager, and are they going to be comfortable with the tenant profile in the location. This will help you create a scale and get some deals done. Keep that in mind when you are thinking about your marketing pieces and testing them out. You can also do a specific flyer for cars in a townhouse complex or just a street itself. This could be a flyer with your name on it, and you can have it delivered to a general area. It is a bit trickier to generate leads through these types of letter campaigns, but they are also much easier to deliver because you are not worried about finding out the names of people, and they are obviously received a lot easier.

**301 Anyplace**

## We Will Buy
## Your Home

### Any Condition

### Quick Closing

### Take Over Payments

Call Quentin
905-XXX-XXXX

**1360 Anyplace**

Dear **Homeowner**,

We are looking to **purchase** one **well kept** townhome through a **private sale** at 1360 Anyplace.

**What We Are Offering You**
. We would like to purchase through a private sale
. You don't need to leave your home for showings and open houses.
. You don't need to do any renovations.

**If you are absolutely serious about selling your home in the next six months.**

. We will complete our purchase through lawyers.

**Please leave your name, phone number, unit number, date you would like to close, and asking price at:**

**905-XXX-XXXX**

The downside, however, is that people throwing these out quickly because there is no reason for them to open and read them? It is possible that they just get thrown out but they can drum up some leads. There are a lot of services that allow you to deliver in a postal code. You can look up a specific street or an area and then come up with the postal code. Then, Canada Post will often deliver to the specific postal codes. So, that could be another approach that you can use for your letter campaign along with a flyer campaign. If the letter does not have an envelope when somebody opens the letter, it will force them to look at it. They may take a glance at this or it may just end in the recycling box.

So, how are you planning on using them? When a seller contacts you, remember to let them do the talking, listen to them, and figure out what they need. Things like the closing date, what type of repairs are required, and how you can offer some flexibility to them. If the home needs repair, make sure that you take it out of whatever the price of the house is, as you are a problem-solver and you want to complete this deal. Make sure that they also get what they need out of it, whatever it is—a quick closing, it is a hoarder house and they do not want to deal with it, or just want to leave everything there. Just add that into your numbers and when they make sense, solve that problem.

When a seller contacts you remember:

- **Let them do the talking.**
- **Figure out what they need in terms of closing date or to leave some repairs for me to do or some other type of flexibility.**
- **If the house needs repairs, I asked them to take it out of the price of the house.**
- **Be a problem-solver and you will be better able to get the deals done.**

So, when I first started out using the strategy of focusing on a specific area, I would not make purchases if I found a property under 15 percent below the market price. You might consider it a strange approach, but in retrospect, I feel like I was being a bit greedy at the time. These were great properties that I could have bought, which were 10 percent below market value and with very few repairs. Now, if I ran into those same types of properties, I would use buy, fix, refinance, and rent strategies. I would pick up those properties any day of the week. I was always going for the home run, instead of picking up the singles, doubles, and triples. If I were to go back again and do anything differently, it would be picking up those singles, doubles, and triples because in the end, if I am buying in a strategic area, with all the fundamentals, getting cash flow on those properties, it all makes sense, I would continue to buy that asset.

Now, make sure that you are using purchase agreements. Make sure that you get all of this in place ahead of time, have them reviewed so that you have the right purchase and sale agreement. Before you start doing your marketing, you want to verify everything and have all your clauses ready. Your lawyer should be able to review all the paperwork and leave it open-ended. This will allow you and your seller's lawyer to be able to review the paperwork. You do not want to put people into a position where you lock them in and you get stuck in this deal. I do not believe that it is an appropriate way of dealing with the sellers. Some people think that is not how I would deal with it. Remember, you are there, and if they think that this is not the right deal for them, then they can walk and move to something else.

If you realize that you got a lead or an opportunity and you lack the confidence to get a private sale done, you have the option to pay a realtor to assist you with the purchase. If you find somebody that you have developed a relationship with over time, you should not ask them to work for free, but you can pay them something like 1 percent or 2 percent of the transaction. They can walk you through the whole thing. Once they help you get through the process a couple of times, you will get the hang of it and you will not need help. Have a lawyer review the paperwork to make sure that everything is in order. They are going to do it anyway because they are going to go through the transaction with you.

I would like to share a few tips here. When you are focusing on a specific area and you are going with the service, I suggest you spot check the delivery the first few times to verify and ensure that it is being delivered. Some services will take pictures of every delivery as they go through it. While you may have to pay a bit more for that type of service, it is worth it. Find out when they will be doing the delivery in your area and then do the spot check. Another option is just hiring a local or hiring a person off Kijiji.

The service will vary depending on who you hire, and I would definitely be spot-checking anybody that I hired that way, but it could be a good way for you to let them make a few extra bucks and you get your flyer delivered. You do not want to be the person who is doing that ten or fifteen dollar an hour job. You want to focus on the leads that are coming in, being ready and handling them. Just make sure that when you are dealing with anybody like that, you pay them when the job is done.

Whether you use them again or not, pay them and then they are out of your hair, and you can move on, or you can use their services again. This strategy is great when you are finding deals on specific streets, and I have been able to use it over the years. I know that there are people who would have paid higher for the same properties that I bought using these types of direct marketing strategies on specific streets. For years, I have had investors ask me how I was able to get the property at that price. It is really up to you to go out and apply that knowledge.

Let us say you find a small list, specific house, or a specific property that you want to get under contract, you can try something that is off the wall and a little different, like a lumpy mail campaign.

## Lumpy Mail

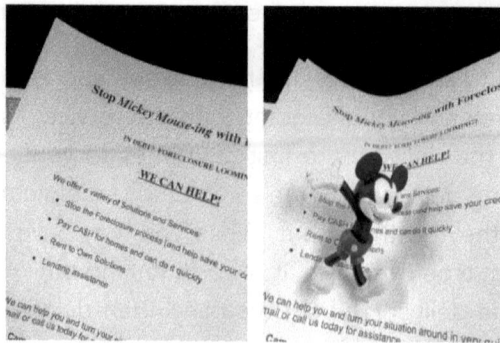

Put something in the letter or envelope that makes it appear lumpy and odd, and whatever it is, you want to make it part of your marketing campaign. Here is an example, a Mickey Mouse figurine or anything similar and you put it in there. It is very targeted and it should not be for 100 or 200 letters that go out, and this is an example from another investor. It is more likely for the potential buyer to open this up. As you are giving something to somebody, you are going to get a response so keep that in mind. This is something just a little out of the box, but it does work, and what you want are strategies that work. Remember, the key is getting out there when you are focusing on a specific area and trying different approaches to getting leads.

# Chapter 12

# Wholesalers

- How I know a big real estate course has come through town is the bunch of new "We Buy Houses For Cash" signs pop up all over the place.
- I often find people who are trying to get into real estate without any money or experience try using wholesaling in order to make some quick cash.
- The challenges that you need to have experience dealing with people and being able to solve problems.
- It takes time and effort in order to learn how to make people comfortable and solve the problem.
- The more deals you have under your belt the easier getting more deals become.

Wholesalers can be a great part of your business. You do not have to be the wholesaler; you can buy from the wholesaler. It takes time and effort to learn how to do that and be comfortable solving problems, and it only happens as you gain experience and get more deals under your belt—that is when it becomes easier.

Wholesaling is a great way to make money, and it does make sense. You can use it in combination with flipping, and it can be an excellent business opportunity. However, you have to remember that it is a business, and it takes time to make it into a business, where you are not in the business all the time. That is really where you want to get to. A lot of people never get to that point in Canada, as we do not have as large of a market as the US. We have a fraction of the market, and it is a much more popular strategy across the border but it can be done in Canada. Do not let anybody tell you, "*It cannot be done.*" It is usually a realtor or person with a poor mindset who has said such things to me in the past. If you have a property under contract, under a purchase and sale agreement, it is assignable in Canada or in Ontario. Even if it does not say that it is assignable, all agreements are assignable, unless it says it is not assignable in the agreement.

## Wholesaling is by no means an easy business to get into.

- **You need to find the discounted properties**
- **You need to be able to negotiate with the seller in order to get those discounted properties.**
- **You also need to negotiate with the seller to show the property to potential buyers.**
- **You need to have buyers list with active buyers that are lined up, have all their financing in order and a ready to buy.**
- **You need to ensure all the proper legal paperwork and purchase agreement terms are completed.**
- **You need to ensure that the deal closes.**

When you assign an agreement you have under contract, that person can pay you an assignment fee for that. It happens in condo buildings all the time. Similarly, before closing on a condo that was under construction, you have often seen people selling assignments for those condo properties. So, you need to find a discounted property and you need to negotiate that. If you are going to do this by yourself, you need to have lead generation, negotiate with the seller, and show the property to potential buyers. You need to have a buyer's list created with active buyers, who are ready to go and have all their financing in place. You need to have all the proper legal paperwork and purchase agreement terms, and you need to ensure that the deal closes. Just remember that you may have an assignment agreement, but until the deal closes, you have not made money.

1. **Assignment agreement with existing purchase agreement**
2. **New purchase agreement with a side assignment agreement**
3. **Amendments with existing purchase agreement.**

There are lots of challenges that come up before closing. So, just because you have not experienced that yet, does not mean it does not exist. There is a lot that goes on in the back end of the wholesaling business. Some people are not great wholesalers, and some are just doing it wrong because they have learned from the wrong people. They could have seen something on YouTube or in the US that they think will apply in Canada.  So the idea behind wholesaling is that somebody is finding a property that is undervalued, and they are assigning that property to you for some sort of an assignment fee, and this fee can range from a few $1,000 to $10,000, or even more depending on the property. I have heard of assignment fees for $100,000 or $200,000, depending on how much of a spread there is in the opportunity.

They use all types of marketing to find those properties and, basically, a wholesaler acts as a middleman and takes a percentage or a property fee amount. I wouldn't call it a percentage because it can vary. There is no particular number. It just depends on the value of the property. Let us say it is $300,000 and after repair, the value is $450,000. Repairs are at a wholesale fee of $20,000, and the property still makes sense to purchase and go through the process, especially if it is a rental. It really does vary from property to property. I have seen wholesale fees that are not really wholesale fees at all, they are actually selling the property at retail price, and that is what makes sense because there is a lot of competition in the market.

Wholesaler: 300k
ARV: 450k
Repairs: 80k

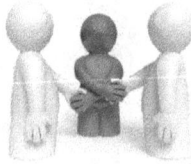

Wholesale Fee: 20K

Wholesaler: 320k
ARV: 450k
Repairs: 80k

There are a few different ways that I see assignments happen. Most of the time, a wholesaler will have a purchase agreement that they have already signed with the seller. Once you get that, you need to create a new purchase and sale agreement, or you have and that means having the new seller agree to the new purchase price and then having a separate assignment agreement, or you have both in some cases. Let us say you are making an amendment to the purchase and sale agreement that removes the wholesaler from the deal and puts yourself in the deal. Again, you have to have trust with that other person, and you have a separate assignment agreement, purchase and sale agreement, or an assignment agreement, and you take that to a lender.

Now, when you are typically working with a bank, they are not going to accept that assignment agreement. You may be able to do an assignment agreement with a lender. A lot of the private lenders will allow that. What you will need to do is close it with a private or B lender and then refinance into an A lender. That is usually the process, and when I say A lender, I am talking about one of the big banks, and a B lender is a home trust or something like that, or somebody you can directly borrow funds from. So, keep that in mind when you are trying to get the financing done on a deal.

## What About Due Diligence?

- **Home inspection**
- **Financing**
- **Competition in the Space**

So, what about your due diligence? I recommend due diligence when you are purchasing an off market property just like you would be doing with a property off the MLS. The problem is that there are a lot of people who are buying from wholesalers now and it is very competitive. I would still suggest you have a home inspection and financing clause if you can, with a wholesaler. The challenge is, if ten other people are trying to get that deal done, it is just not going to happen. Now, you can eliminate the financing clause by having financing in place. It could be private lending, but if you try to get a lender financing with the wholesaler, they are not going to be too keen on waiting for the process to complete when they can move on to the next person who can pay the same price without the same conditions.

There is a lot of competition in this space, but you need to be careful because you do not want to get into a position where you are purchasing something wholesale, and you are not able to do the work you thought you could. For instance, let us say you are buying a property and you are going to do a basement conversion, and it looks great. Then, you find out that there is a floodplain, and in the floodplain, you are not allowed to do any more additional work to it. Well, if that is the case, then you know that it is not working out in your favor. So, that is also something to be mindful of when looking at a property.

What does an assignment of contract look like? There is a separate assignment of the contract. It is an agreement between you and a person, that they are going to close on the property, and they are agreeing to close on it. Sometimes, you can have assignment agreements where you are going to pay them $100,000 upfront and whatever the balance of the assignment is later. Whatever that number is, you can put that agreement in the assignment of the contract. This is different from a purchase and sale amendment, where you are just taking the purchase and sale agreement and putting your name in there instead of the original purchaser. This assignment contract is a separate agreement altogether. Usually what happens is that you pay the wholesaler directly, you are not going through a lawyer. That is traditionally how I have done it. I am sure that there are other ways to do it, but you can see the typical agreement here now.

## ASSIGNMENT OF CONTRACT

FOR VALUE AGREED UPON, $ 5,000 (Five thousand), the undersigned Assignor **Wholesaler** ("Assignor") hereby agrees and assigns, transfers and sets over to ___**Investor**___ ("Assignee") all rights, title and interest held by the Assignor in and to the following described contract:

Property located at: **123 First Street, Whitby, Ontario**

Agreement of Purchase and Sale dated: **April 26, 2014**

Purchase Price: **$200,000**

The Assignor warrants and represents that said contract is in full force and effect and is fully assignable;

The Assignee hereby assumes and agrees to perform all the remaining and executory obligations of the Assignor under the contract and agrees to indemnify and hold the Assignor harmless from any claim or demand resulting from non-performance by the Assignee;

The Assignee shall be entitled to all monies remaining to be paid under the contract, which rights are also assigned hereunder;

The Assignor warrants that the contract is without modification, and remains on the terms contained;

The Assignor further warrants that it has full right and authority to transfer said contract and that the contract rights herein transferred are free encumbrance or adverse claim;

The undersigned Assignee agrees to pay **Wholesaler** in full all fees, payments or money owed regarding the aforementioned property on or before or within 2 business days of the property closing date;

This assignment shall be binding upon and inure to the benefit of the parties, their successors and assigns.

Signed this __26__ day of ___**April**_____, **2014.**


_____                    _____

Assignor's Signature                       Assignor's Printed Name


_____                    _____

Assignee's Signature                       Assignee's Printed Name

The wholesaling business is an active real estate business. It forces you to continue to funnel new leads and constantly build your buyer's list so you can continue to do what you are doing. This is done on an ongoing basis. This is not passive. It is not passive, no matter what anybody tells you, especially when you are starting. As you grow your business and you have different levels of people that can help you, then you start to remove yourself slowly from it, but it is a very active business. There are some people who are successful at wholesaling, but I have met thousands of investors who have tried and only a handful of successful wholesalers. So, if you are not doing this but you are still interested in real estate, you should probably focus on becoming a realtor. Anyways, that is a different story.

In fact, I would rather purchase a property from a wholesaler and pay a wholesaler fee, as long as there is enough profit in the deal for it to make sense to me. That is why I love to buy assignments from wholesalers. The challenge, of course, is in a competitive market.

So one of the strategies I use is that I call anybody that has posted "We Buy Houses" signs, and I'd let them know, "Hey, look, I have seen your sign," especially if it is an area that I am already interested in, drive around the area and call the signs. That is a great way of doing it. Just make sure that you are calling those people and letting them know, "Look, I buy assignments, so please put me on your buyer's list."

When I see "We Buy Houses" signs online, I will contact people. Especially online, it is an easy and low barrier of entry because of the cost point. You will see a lot of people, who are posting on there, and I usually do not find them great lead sources, but it is a good way to at least get your name out there. Put yourself on different lists. If you are seeing advertisements, you want to connect with them. You can also do searches online to see what comes up. You can connect with people online quite easily through Facebook groups. I find that this is a great way of connecting with other people who are wholesaling properties. I just find that there seems to be a lot more people advertising that they are wholesaling properties when wholesaling properties really seems like just collecting email addresses.

Another great place to find wholesalers is to come out to real estate networking events. I host events every month at Durham-REI.ca. It is a great way to connect with people and find out who the active investors and the active wholesalers are. Some people say that they are wholesaling and never wholesale a single deal. I find that there are a lot of people who do not do what they say. So, you can connect with people at those events that are actually doing what they say. Let them know that you are an active investor and touch base with them every few months. Share your buying criteria with them as well as if it has changed, that way if anything comes up, you have that connection going and you can possibly get a deal done.

I am going to give you an example, and this is an older example of a wholesaler package. It is just a good idea to give you a sense of what you may or may not get from a potential wholesaler. Sometimes, you will get a package of pictures as well. Just make sure you understand what the criteria are, the location of the property that you want to buy, and if you are comfortable enough to move forward with the purchase or not. Just be careful that if you say you are going to do something and do not do it, you will never work with that wholesaler again. So, be a person who is known as a closer, someone who can be relied upon to close on a deal or opportunity. I think that is the key, and you can ask yourself some questions: How could you tell if this was a good opportunity or not and what are the criteria to look for? Does the property match the criteria and in particular, I am referring to this package. So, take some time, take a look at the example and then see price point-wise. Nowadays that makes sense every day, but this gives you a bit of an example of what you might see in a particular wholesaling package.

**Quick Analysis...**
**Whitby, ON Townhouse Under Contract for**
**$105,500** → comparable to 2002 prices!

# 22% below market value

## Table of Contents

Quick Summary: ..................................................................................................... 2
Suggested Exit Strategies: ........................................................................................ 2
Property Details: ....................................................................................................... 2
Cosmetic Renovations Required: ............................................................................. 3
Assignment Fee: ....................................................................................................... 3
MLS Sold Comparables in the area: ........................................................................ 3

## Quick Summary:

- This property is ready for a buy, fix, sell that can make profit quickly OR a buy, fix, rent that will make you income.
- The property can be purchased for $109,000 ($105,500 + $3,500).
- To sell fast, a good listing price is $139,900 and a good sale price is $135,000 to $140,000.
- Material costs for renovations can be as low as $3,000. The main cost will be flooring which could cost you $1/sqft or $5/sqft... it's your choice.
- The renovations could be done by one person in 2-3 weeks.
- Depending on transaction costs, holding costs, financing costs, renovation costs, and sale price... PROFITS of $12,000 to $20,000 will go in your pocket.

### BONUSES:

- Don Campbell and Real Estate Investment Network (REIN) rank Whitby at #3 in its research report of The Top 10 Ontario Towns To Invest In.
- In today's economy, starter homes are selling much better than high-end homes. Many people are also downsizing. This property can sell FAST at the right price.
- This is the LOWEST PRICED HOUSE IN ALL OF WHITBY! And it will still be the lowest priced house when selling for $139,900. Please take a look on MLS to verify this.

## Suggested Exit Strategies:

- Light Rehab – buy, fix, sell
- Rental property – Buy, pretty-up, rent

## Property Details:

- Condo townhouse at 101 Dovedale Dr in Whitby (close to Dundas & Garden)
- 1100 sq ft
- 30 to 40 years old
- 3 bed, 1 bath
- two storey with partially finished basement

## Cosmetic Renovations Required:

- interior painting of entire house
- replace all carpet
- install flooring in basement
- new paneling and drop ceiling in basement
- fix screen door, replace kitchen counter
- needs cleaning and other touch-ups

## Assignment Fee: $3500

The property is under contract for $105,500 and no further negotiations are needed. Closing Date is November 05, 2008

## MLS Sold Comparables in the area:

109 Dovedale Dr unit 48, 7/1/2008, $149,000
101 Dovedale Dr unit 2, 12/4/2007, $122,000  (NOTE: this was a Power Of Sale, so not representative of a renovated property.)
105 Dovedale Dr unit 9, 8/18/2007, $129,000
105 Dovedale Dr unit 6, 7/28/2007, $125,900
109 Dovedale Dr unit 47, 6/1/2007, $140,000
107 Dovedale Dr unit 57, 6/22/2007, $141,000
103 Dovedale Dr unit 22, 4/24/2007, $132,000
107 Dovedale Dr unit 59, 12/6/2006, $135,250
101 Dovedale Dr unit 24, 10/12/2006, $138,000
NOTE: $136,000 is a conservative after rehab sale price.  House prices vary depending on how nice the renovations are.

Photos, MLS Comparables, and further details are available.

# Chapter 13

# The Lead Sheet

I know it seems simple, but this is an example of a lead generation sheet. If you are not going to use a lead sheet, then you want to use a program like Call Rail to keep everything online for the leads that come in or some other CRM type of system. Whether it is Active Campaign, Zolo, Hubspot, or whatever system that you have or you want to use, you want to be able to track every single lead that comes in.

There are a few things that you want to know right away. So, if you look at this sheet, you will see that it covers information such as: How did you hear about us? This is the first question because I want to know how I got my lead into my funnel because then I know what is working and what is not. There is office use only, lead number, what the lead is, and the date and the time it was called because I want to make sure that it is followed up at the right time.

You will want to get the name of the person and phone numbers, and all of this has to be conversational. The address of the property, city, location, is the property already listed on the MLS? You want to ask that right away because it may just make this not useful for you. If it is listed, you ask who it is listed with, that way you can keep track of it, especially if you are seeing patterns.

**FDP Lead Sheet**

Office Use Only

Lead No.: _____  Date: _____ /20____  Time: _____ AM / PM

How did you hear about us? _____

Name: _____ Phone # 1: (____) _____ Phone # 2: (____) _____

Property Address: _____ City: _____ Prov.: _____

City / Town: _____ Neighbourhood: _____

Is the property currently listed for sale? ☐ Yes ☐ No   If Yes, with whom? _____

When would you like to move? _____

Property Type: ☐ Condominium ☐ Single Family ☐ Bungalow ☐ 2-Storey ☐ Split Level ☐ Bi-Level ☐ Duplex ☐ Townhouse

Sq-Ft: _____   No. of Bedrooms: _____   No. of Bathrooms: _____   Age: _____ ☐ Carport ☐ Garage ☐ None

Does the property require any repairs? ☐ Yes ☐ No   If Yes, provide details: _____

Upgrades or Special Features: _____

If you don't mind me asking, why are you selling your home? _____

What do you think your home is worth? $_____

How did you arrive at this value? _____

What is the least amount you would accept with an "all-cash" offer? $_____

**If Seller wants FULL Market Value for their Home – Ask for VTB**

**\*\* If there is NO Motivation and NO Terms – STOP Right Here \*\***

**If Terms ARE Available – PROCEED to Collect Additional Information**

1st Mortgage Balance: $_____   Lender: _____   Mortgage Maturity Date: _____

1st Mortgage Payment: $_____   Payments Current: ☐ Yes ☐ No   If No, provide info: _____ /$_____

2nd Mortgage Balance: $_____   Lender: _____   Mortgage Maturity Date: _____

2nd Mortgage Payment: $_____   Payments Current: ☐ Yes ☐ No   If No, provide info: _____ /$_____

Interest Rate 1st Mortgage: _____%   Interest Rate 2nd Mortgage: _____%   _____

Does the mortgage payment include taxes? ☐ Yes ☐ No   If No, what are the property taxes? $_____

If behind on payments, has foreclosure notice been served? ☐ Yes ☐ No   If Yes, provide details: _____

Are there any liens, caveats or other items secured against the property? ☐ Yes ☐ No   _____

Other (property or situation) Information: _____

**Remember: NEVER Leave Your Chair at Home to Go Look at a Property...Unless You have a COMPELLING Reason to Do So!**

This Property Does Not Meet Me Criteria But I Can Give This Lead to : _____

DurhamREI Coaching and Mastermind Program          ©DREIC Publishing 2015

Then, what is the property type square footage? Are there any repairs? Sometimes, they will say that there are no repairs, and when you visit the property, it needs a ton of repairs. So, first you want to find out what they are from their perspective. If you can get pictures that would be even better, is there anything unique or special about the property? Then find out their motivation. Why are they selling? Are they getting a divorce? Are they moving? When do they want to move? What is the reason for it? And then ask them what they think about the value of their property and what they want to sell it for. Then, how did they come up with that value? Did they get that number from a neighbor who sold a similar property? Is there a number that they have in mind and if you could close cash right away? What is the "as is" cash price for the property? What will they accept?

Sometimes the deal makes sense right away, and if you were to give them their full asking price, specifically apartment building owners, you can ask for a vendor take-back mortgage. The apartment building owners are more sophisticated and understand it. Essentially, it is a term in your agreement where the seller is holding back, like a first or a second mortgage on the property, and with specific terms like 5 percent interest only for three years. By doing that, they can defer their capital gains for a couple of years and perhaps make some changes to their lifestyle to lessen the tax hit. But at this point, you should have an idea of whether there is motivation. You can get some terms on the property, and if there is nothing that makes sense at this point, then you may not want to continue.

I would suggest, though, that you can proceed with collecting some additional information, especially if it is the first time you want to talk about the mortgage, the lender, the due date, any second mortgage. This type of information can help you find out whether they are behind on their mortgages or not. How far behind are they? Have they been served any documentation around "for foreclosure" or "power of sale?" Are there any other caveats against the property, like a construction loan or something similar? Maybe there is something they do not know about. It could be past property taxes or other priority liens. Is there any information about the situation that you can come up with from the conversation with the particular seller? You will see how motivated someone is by the information they are willing to give you.

**My rule is never to leave your chair. Never go see the property unless there is a compelling reason to do so.** You want to have that compelling reason to do so, otherwise, you are wasting your time traveling all over the place.

If the property does not meet your criteria, who are you going to give the lead to? You do not want it to go to anything, but you do want to try to convert it. So, write it down, make sure that you send it and get the information to the person who might be interested. Now, let us say you get the property and you have a purchase price, the renovation price, and the fair market value or aftermarket value. If you are going to hold it, what is the potential rent, mortgage property taxes, insurance, and utilities? What do you think would be the cash flow on it? If you are getting terms, you need to get a joint venture, RRSP mortgage, or a vendor take-back mortgage. What are those terms? That is going to help you to evaluate whether this deal makes sense.

What about the zoning or location? Does the zoning allow you to take it from a single-family home up to a triplex? Is the location really desirable? Maybe by the lake, where you can do some extra work to the property and then it would be worth something even more? All of these things are important for you to be able to figure out what you are going to do with this property and analyze it. When you get to the property, you would get an estimate of the different repairs. This comes from experience. It can be something electronic, but if you know what it is going to cost you to do a roof in the area, maybe about $5,000, downspouts, gutters $2,000, and what really needs to be done in the property, then you will have an estimate. What if there are other things? You develop this over time, and you can come up with an idea of the renovation costs or repairs, and that will give you a good idea of whether this is actually going to be a deal or not.

## FDP Analysis Sheet

Project Title: _____

| HIGHEST AND BEST USE | PROPERTY LOCATION | SELLER FINANCING | PRICE | CONDITION OF THE PROPERTY | TOTAL SCORE |
|---|---|---|---|---|---|
| ★★ | ★★ | ★★★ | ★★★ | ★★★ | |

Purchase Price: _____  Repairs and Renovations: _____  Final Market Value: _____

| HOLD | |
|---|---|
| Potential Rent | |
| Mortgage(s) | |
| Property Taxes | |
| Insurances | |
| Utilities/Fees | |
| Cash Flow (+/-) | |

| TERMS | |
|---|---|
| VTB | |
| RRSP Mortgages | |
| JV Agreement | |
| Other Terms | |

| HIDDEN GEMS | |
|---|---|
| ZONING | |
| LOCATION | |
| OTHER | |

| REPAIRS AND RENOVATIONS | | | |
|---|---|---|---|
| Exterior | Estimate | Kitchen | Estimate |
| Roof | | Cabinets | |
| Gutters & Downspouts | | Cabinet Knobs | |
| Front Door Light | | Counter Tops | |
| Exterior Painting | | Sink | |
| House Number | | Taps | |
| Mail Box | | Appliances | |
| Front Door | | Plumbing | |
| Locks | | Electrical | |
| Window & Doors | | Drywall | |
| Landscaping | | Backsplash | |
| Siding | | Lighting | |
| Deck and Porch | | Flooring | |
| Foundations | | Overall Interior | Estimate |
| Garage | | Paint - Walls | |
| Bathroom | Estimate | Trims | |
| Tub and Toilet | | Door Handles | |
| Sink | | Closet Knobs | |
| Cabinet | | Light Switches & Plugs | |
| Cabinet Knobs | | Floor & Fresh Air Vents | |
| Counter Top | | Floor Coverings | |
| Tiles or Tub Surround | | Light Fixtures | |
| Towel Bar & T.P Holder | | Electrical | |
| Plumbing | | Drywall | |
| Electrical | | Lighting | |
| Drywall | | Flooring | |
| Lighting | | Basement | Estimate |
| Flooring | | Furnace | |
| Drywall | | Hot Water Tank | |
| Subtotal | | Moisture Issues | |
| TOTAL | | Subtotal | |

### HOW CAN I PROFIT FROM THIS PROPERTY?

☐Joint Venture ☐Assign the Property ☐Flip ☐Buy,Fix,Refinance,and Rent ☐Buy and Hold ☐Lease Option ☐ Sandwich Lease ☐ AFS

BONUS: ☐Lots of Built-In Equity ☐ Quick Repairs ☐ Renovations wil Raise Equity Significantly

DurhamREI Coaching and Mastermind Program          ©DREIC Publishing 2015

You are going to miss things, and that is why you go back with a contractor for your home inspection, then include that in your purchase and sale agreement. This or a similar lead sheet gives you a good idea of whether this property is worthwhile or not.

Now, I have a star system that I used when I was doing the single-family to a one-, two-, or three-unit type of space, but this type of sheet is useful. You should have some variation of it, either on paper or online. One of the things that I would give to my coaching clients, also thinking about how they are going to profit from the property, remember, you need to have multiple exit strategies—**always, always, always** have multiple exit strategies.

If you are not going to be able to flip it, can you hold on to it? If you are going to hold on to it, can you do a new joint venture with somebody? Can you create a lease option on it? Do you need to do a sandwich lease? There are all these creative strategies, and you need to develop your toolbox so that you can handle them. Then, once you can handle them, this becomes part of your infrastructure and part of your off market and discounted properties system. That is how you are going to build out and you are going to use this tool as part of the next phase, and we are going to get into it—the marketing pieces.

# Chapter 14

# Offline Print Marketing

I am going to go through both offline marketing and online marketing. While I can not cover everything there is to know about offline and online marketing in this book, I will share the top 10–20 percent of information that you need to get started and go down the right path. Read this book, and take this chapter as a starting point to get you in the right direction about marketing.

## Magazine, Newspapers, Classified Ads and More

- **Marketing is a very important part of your real estate business; in fact I don't know of a business where marketing isn't integral.**

- **For you it may just mean advertising to find properties at a discount, but it could also mean building great ads to attract high quality tenants, to find good tenant-buyers, or to find buyers of properties that you decide to sell. Whatever the case may be there are lots of great resources where you can learn about marketing.**

Offline print marketing—you might be asking—print marketing, do people still do that? The answer is, yes. Do you need to do it? Not necessarily. Should you perhaps try it? Probably. You need to find what works for you. You can be different, or you can be the same as other people who are marketing for properties. However you do it, it has to be comfortable for you.

When you are thinking about offline marketing, it is really important to first understand that it is part of your business. I do not know a business that is not marketing. You have to do that to bring leads in and bring new business to yourself. When you are marketing or advertising for properties, it is more than bringing in just a discounted property—it is about finding the right person. It helps to filter out those people that do not meet your criteria, those people who want to get top dollar for their property, or it is a way for you and your marketing to get the good-quality talent tenants and avoid low-quality tenants. The idea behind marketing is that it acts as a filter and brings in the leads. That is what you want to do, and that is what we are going to talk about here.

I want to start with some suggestions. I am going to include some resources in the material below. Some of my favorite authors are Dan Kennedy, Jay Abraham, and Robert Cialdini, and it is well worth your time doing a deep dive into marketing and reading books by these authors. It will help you tweak your advertising so that you can continue to improve. You might come up with different strategies just by reading about the strategies that nobody else is using right now, and that is how you differentiate yourself, but do not take this as *"this is what you do."* Continue to learn and continue to grow. You can do some amazing deals if you can generate the right leads.

Let us talk a little bit more about some offline print marketing. There are lots of places that you can go to find interesting opportunities. In your local area, you might have one of those property or real estate magazines. Remember to think about who the clientele is that is going to pick up those magazines. It is going to be people who are probably looking for a property that is their first one or perhaps they are selling their first property.

**Check out the real estate magazines in your local area you never know what type of properties you will find. One example is Homes and Land of the Durham Region.**

**This glossy magazine is example of a free magazine that you can find in paper boxes at the corner of some intersections, and malls, coffee shops, and various stores.**

**Other examples of print editions in my area are Ajax Your Local Real Estate, North Durham New and Resale Homes Port Perry, Uxbridge & Beyond, Oshawa Real Estate, and Cobourg Port Hope and Surrounding Area Real Estate.**

There could be higher-end magazines and you are going to have higher-end homes that appear in them. You want to examine the magazines as you never know what opportunities you might find. Pick up those glossy free magazines and go through them. You could even contact people from there. Do not limit yourself to thinking that MLS is the only way to find opportunities. You might find some pocket listings in there. You might connect with a realtor who has some interesting opportunities. Look in your area, you might have different print editions of these magazines that are for your specific town, region, or surrounding area. Whatever that is, you want to take the time to be able to go out and use these magazines. Some of these magazines are widely distributed across Canada, and the *Real Estate Book* is one.

Sometimes, you can find interesting multifamily opportunities in those magazines. Perhaps they are not listed on the typical websites like MLS, and there are pocket listings. As you find them in these real estate books, it is a little different than what other people are looking for, and you are spending that extra time to utilize other resources to bring leads to yourself. This is not actually print marketing; it is just looking at other people's marketing. So, consider that as a different way of bringing in some opportunities to yourself.

What about your marketing? Before we even do that, what about the news advertisers, people publishing "for sale" ads on Metro Land local newspapers, in their classified section. It could be any other major newspaper, as it is not really the fact that it is listed there but who is the person that is listing a property in a newspaper. They are going to be an interesting clientele. Think about it, who might be a person that does not list online but lists in a newspaper. That might give you an idea of the type of clientele that you would be working with.

Finding classified ads in the newspaper might be an opportunity for you to get a new deal. The other thing is, the way that we have been looking at this, at this point, is where we are waiting for deals to appear. We are looking at newspapers, we are looking at magazines, and we are contacting realtors that might have pocket listings. So, that means being a bit more proactive, but for the most part, we were quite passive. Depending on the clientele that you are going to be attracting or looking for in the magazines and newspapers, I would say it is probably an older clientele. You just have to keep that in mind when you are talking with the potential leads that come from this.

What about actually advertising yourself? Perhaps trying out advertising in the print media, you never know. I have not done that in a very long time, but maybe just to distinguish yourself. It does not have to be as you might think, putting in an advertise-ment with a gripping headline, "*I will buy your house fast,*" and maybe a little clip art image, something that sets you apart, "*No commission, any condition, no equity, no problem.*" Remember, you are a problem-solver so add something along those lines. Then, add a way for them to contact you—your number, website information, includes it in your call to action. Creating it does not have to be too complex. Let us say we were doing some samples of an advertisement, something simple.

Develop a few ads for yourself, what could you do? What kind of ads can you come up with? Whatever method of advertising you use, whether it is newspaper advertising or online advertising that we will be talking about later — you always need to track your results. You can add a dedicated phone number, dedicated URL to a website, so you need to track the results. Start with advertising in a magazine and then track the results. When a newspaper attracts the results, maybe try different headlines, see what works and what does not. You could try different newspapers in different areas, do a test run and see what you get. You can tweak the advertising, and whatever you do in offline print advertising, you could do in online advertising.

So, the idea is that no matter what type of advertising you do, you always want to track the results, and when you find something that is working, do not change it, keep at it, until it does not work anymore. Then, test other ads; change your formula, but only when it stops working. As long as it keeps generating leads, it is a good marketing formula.

So, let us take this a little bit further. One thing that you may want to consider with your advertising, and something that I have not done, but would be interesting, is to offer to purchase properties with a large portfolio. Offer to buy several properties at once, in order to "Buy Wholesale." Then, perhaps you could sell a few of those properties off to other investors "At Retail" and use the funds that you get to pay down some of the other properties. That is a great way of going about it. Depending on the circulation of the magazine and who it is appealing to, you could try posting an advertisement in it. There are lots of other ideas, but these are just a couple of brainstorming pieces here around offline print marketing and how you can use them for lead generation.

# Chapter 15

# Online Marketing

This is a huge chapter for you, and this is really just the tip of the iceberg like offline marketing. If you really want to do well in real estate, you need to spend time working on it.

The internet has made things much easier for everybody when it comes to connecting buyers and sellers. It helps them connect directly with each other. Love it or hate it, the internet is here to stay and the available services are not going away either. I know that there are a lot of realtor organizations that keep pushing to fight it, but we know that things are changing. A good example is what is happening in the US, and really what we are seeing is innovation. This makes things better for both buyers and sellers. There are different ways that you can do a transaction that is not based on the MLS. Just like what iTunes did for music, we are seeing innovations appear in the real estate space, particularly in apps and things that can be helpful but also, like I said, connecting buyers and sellers directly together.

These new online systems are useful for real estate investors who are not realtors. I see this change as an opportunity here, but you still need to do all the proper due diligence on the purchase and sale. If you have not ever purchased a property before, I suggest you still go through a realtor, especially if this is your very first purchase. You really want to have somebody to guide you through the process, and also having a good team around you means having a good realtor with you. At the very least, you need to work with your lawyer to go through your contract and make sure that everything is moving in the right direction. After the details, the sale price and the terms are agreed upon. It is the lawyer that usually handles everything from then on to the closing. You want to make sure that you have a lawyer that is experienced in real estate transactions, particularly with clauses and how things work within your purchase agreement.

There are lots of opportunities to use online marketing, but just be cautious about what you are doing online and what you are purchasing online.

- **New online systems are useful tools for real estate investors, who are not realtors.**
- **Always do your due diligence on the purchase and sale.**
- **Always have all your documents reviewed by a highly experienced real estate focused lawyer before you sign anything and include it in your purchase agreement.**
- **There are plenty of opportunities using online marketing, but make sure that you are cautious about the purchases and sales that you do online.**

There are easy ways to get started that do not cost a lot of money. They may not be as effective as other methods, but it is worthwhile, at least starting in that direction. An easy way to start is to look at properties that are available on Kijiji, Craigslist, and any online forum that is not the MLS or realtor.ca. That way you can see if there are any off market properties and find out what is the motivation of the people who are selling. The main difference between working directly with a seller and working with a third party that intermediates is that you often do not get the motivation of the seller. What do they need to solve? Are they moving to another state or country? Is there something that is going on that requires them to sell, like a divorce or any other situation? This is the type of information that you can use to help you make the offer more appealing to a seller. I recall going between a husband and wife in a divorce situation and getting documents signed because it was just easier to do if I did it, versus them doing it together. They agreed to the price but they didn't want to see each other. So, finding out that motivation will be helpful for you when you are getting things done.

Other ways of looking are moving sales or garage sales online. Sometimes, when you are looking at these sales, when the contents are being removed, it is probably because they are going to be selling their property. It could be one of the reasons and that they are selling soon. Asking never hurts. **If you are not going to do something different, you are not going to get any different results.** So, that is something that you can do. While it is a bit different and not quite the same as somebody posting online that they are looking to sell their house, it is still easily accessible.

I have come across some interesting deals just by talking to other people who are selling online. I had a situation where it was a landlord who had just evicted their tenant and was trying to sell the property. It was a lead from Craigslist. I am sharing this from my personal experience of buying properties this way. So, the landlord was busy, a small business owner and the house needed some small repairs, nothing too dramatic, and we were able to get the house. It didn't cost a lot to fix it up. Then, we were able to refinance the property one year later. Property next door was sold for a little bit more, which worked out well for us, and it all started from a conversation through Craigslist. Although Craigslist is not the same as it was before, it is still just going out of your comfort zone and trying a different approach—that is what is going to help you, not surfing sites like realtor.ca.

What about advertising on these websites? Kijiji, Craigslist, offer services of buying and selling properties online. If you are somebody who has a "We Buy Houses" type of approach, perhaps you can post that online, or you can contact people who have those services online and see if they would assign you properties. It could be a simple ad on a website, and it does not have to cost a lot to connect or refer you to someone else. Whenever you make a contact, you want to also say, *"Hey, listen, if you do not have a property, if you refer somebody to me with whom I can close on the property, I am happy to pay you a referral fee."*

Whatever that referral fee is, you want to follow the rules of the online website, but you also want to track the results of your ads. Whatever you change or do in your advertising, you want to track the results, as you want to see what is working, what is not. Often, it is as easy as just changing the email address associated with the ad. If you use a web hosting provider, oftentimes, you can have your domain name with multiple email addresses, and you can add different websites, whatever your URL is, and you can track your advertising and your results. That way, you will always be able to figure out where everything's coming up from because then you can focus your time and energy on what is working and eliminate what is not

## Advertising on Craigslist/Kijiji/Other Sites:

Placing a simple ad on these websites might provide you with a lead that will help you to purchase your next discounted investment property or help you to connect with someone who refers someone else to you. Follow the rules of the website and track the results of your ads. Google's great for that—you can use little tricks on Google to change your email address and make it easier for you to track by creating slight variations of the email address. If you have a + sign and your name@gmail.com, you are still going to get that email to come to your name+specificuse@gmail.com. Here are some examples of how that works. I have a Gmail account, let's say it is quentin@gmail.com. You can use variations by putting periods in between your name and/or using your quentin+kijiji@gmail.com or q.uentin@gmail.com and using the plus sign or period you get your emails sent to you. There are just a few tricks that you can learn, and they may change over time, which help you to track your leads.

You will have to experiment and test this out to see whether it works, but really, it is all about testing. Online marketing is about trialing, retesting, and seeing what brings in results, and then focusing on it. So, once you set up a search, you can search for any email address that you use in your Gmail account and the results you are getting. So, just make sure to sign up to one online service, with one unique email address, like: Kijiji, one email address, Craigslist, one email address, any other online service, separate email addresses—that way you can track it and, oftentimes, your username and password can be saved in your browser. It is all about trying to figure out what works and what does not.

> *TIP: Once you set this up, you can search for any email address that you used in your Gmail account and see what type of results you are getting. Just make sure to sign up for the online services with unique email addresses.*

Writing your ads, there are simple, easy-to-the-point ways of advertising. You have to remember that with online advertising, you are capturing their attention based on the subject line. If you are looking to capture somebody's interest, you want to say something like "We Buy Houses," "House Collector," or something that draws their attention and has them click on the link. Once they click on the link, you want to be direct about your offer. You can have some general online advertising, but you want to quickly connect with somebody or have somebody call or text right away. That way you can connect with them and, hopefully, call them back and find an interesting opportunity.

One thing that I see a lot of is, *"We buy houses fast and for cash, any condition, any problem. You can sell your home quickly at no cost to you and no harm to your credit. So, basically, we are saying that there are no additional fees that are associated with it. Even if you have a bit of equity, or no equity, or even negative equity, we are able to help you."*

There are different strategies that you can use when you are working with somebody with no equity or little equity. It takes a bit more effort, and you will have to look up what agreement for sale and other strategies are, but the goal is to solve problems for somebody else so that they can sell their house. That is what we want to be able to do.

We Buy Houses !!

You have a property...
And we have CASH!
How about we trade?!

CA$H REWARD
Up to $2,000
Referral money for you
On closing

Call or Text 416-xxx-xxxx

As you gain more experience, you will be able to do what you want to do. Depending on whatever the situation is, you can usually work it out. I have had realtors contact me because they just want to sell the property but are having some issues. Whether the problem or situation where I was able to offer a solution to the homeowner, the realtor still got their commission. I was able to buy the house because it made sense.

We are looking for homes with motivated sellers. I am not a real estate agent. Again, this is an example of advertising:

*"I am only looking for older homes, in original condition, that are ready to be updated and renovated. Sorry, no knockdowns. If you are looking to move and your house is long in the tooth, and you do not have the time or means to update—I want your home, quick closings with no conditions. Market values would be paid with no realtor fees. This is cash in your pocket. We are ready to buy. Are you ready to sell again?"*

You are engaging people with what you are talking about and hopefully inspiring them to connect with you. You want them to connect with you as quickly as you can.

With online advertising, you want to quickly gain their attention and get them to call you. That is the whole point of this practice. Some types of advertising that are kind of interesting are, *"This is the type of property that we are interested in. This is the price range we are interested in. If you are interested and have a property like this, call us. We are offering a service, and we want to buy that property from you."* Again, examples of locations, trying to be as specific as possible, and if those people meet our criteria, we are filtering them down. When they contact us, do we have the right people? Remember, by being more specific, you have to sort through fewer properties and appeal directly to the type of buyer you want.

Make sure that you are truthfully advertising online. You want to convey to people that you are going to do what you say you are going to do. You do not want to over-promise and under-deliver—that is not good. It is better that instead of wasting time, you find the right person, and you want to help them so that you can create a win-win situation. They get to sell their property and you get a little bit of a discount. Online advertising is great, but I do not think it is the only means that you should be connecting with potential buyers. This is just one of the ways to do it. Now, the most important part of online marketing is having a place for people to go to. At the very least, you must have a phone number and email address.

One thing that I suggest, even if you are not technically inclined, I am going to give you a solution to attract potential property sellers, advertising in different places, perhaps Google ads, Facebook ads, whatever you choose to work on. At least have a phone number, but having a website where people can fill out a form or download something and connect with you is much better. They are looking online because they are looking for a specific solution. You want to make sure that you offer them one. You do not have to explain it all, but the website should show examples of how you can solve their problems.

I want you to have a look at the Carrot Real Estate Investor website. I am going to show you plenty of examples of where other investors have gone to create lead generation websites. This is the website that I use to create lead generation for my website. I bring everything from different places through my Investor Carrot website. We will look at that in detail in the next chapter, but I wanted to give you a chance to explore it. If you are serious about online lead generation, my suggestion is to sign up for something like this. Do not waste your time trying to reinvent the wheel. If you are very skilled at website development, you understand WordPress, and can do the online marketing piece, then what I suggest is to do it yourself, but for those of you that are not, I suggest you take a look at Investor Carrot as a solution for you (www. carrot.com).

# Chapter 16

# Online Marketing

We are still talking about the marketing for off market properties. We are focusing on websites and looking at things that stand out about them. Now, I am going to upset a couple of my friends because I am going to mess up some of their tracking numbers. After all, we are going to have a lot of people who go to their website but they will not know where the lead came from. To be fair, I am doing it on my own website as well. I am not as heavily invested in marketing in the online space in the one to four units anymore. I am doing things a bit differently, but I want to share some examples and talk more about this. Here are a few websites, let us take a look at the websites themselves.

- **https://www.webuyhousescash.ca/**
- **https://www.gtahousebuyers.ca/**
- **https://www.ibuyhousestoronto.ca/**
- **https://416homebuyer.ca/**

So, "We Buy Houses Cash" is my website. If you go to it, you will be able to see that there is a theme around all these websites. One is you can see here, *"Sell your house quick, fair price, put your name in, let us get it done quickly, and we will give you a fair price."* You will see that I am directing you to specific areas, you can go through the process. What about if you are avoiding power sales or foreclosures, which I have purchased before, through my own website, some examples of testimonials. When you go through this, what you are going to notice is Investor Carrot. I did not make my own website.

There should be a few things that you are going to notice there: "Satisfaction guarantee, no obligation," etc. You will notice some testimonials, things that make you a little different and also connect you with the person. Like I have said, I am not marketing as heavily in this way anymore, but I still have this website up because I do get the occasional lead that comes through. It is from previous posts or something that I put online, and I am getting connections in the lead that comes from it.

Here is another one from another friend of mine. What you will notice here is that he has his accredited business status, a Better Business Bureau rating. If you click on it, it actually takes you there. You will notice that you can go through the website. What Aaron does really well is that he is showing people who he is, and he is creating a connection with them. Aaron is a really smart man and a great guy, too, but you can see with the type of connections he has, as well as videos of people selling him properties. He has marketing pages for each of the areas that he is working on and, again, Investor Carrot, but he does a great job. Let us see what his contact looks like. So, he has an address and phone number information and he has a free download, Stop the Foreclosure guide, where he has answered some frequently asked questions, as well as his testimonials. This is an effective approach to presenting content on a website It has several great testimonials and videos. Hearing from different clients that he has helped mention his name directly adds to his credibility. You will notice, though, that every time you go to the front page of the website, the same thing that I have—address, phone number, and email to help you get connected quickly.

## Use Other Visitors to Help Legitimate Your Service or Website:

- A little trick I use is to have a service like Proof or Trust Pulse to let visitors know that your site is being used by other people.
- People will not call you if they do not trust you. These services are an easy way to add authenticity to your offering.
- Other ways to do this: show testimonials, share information about your team, let people know who you are with photos and bios.

Let us take a look at another one. I recognize the branding there for Luc and he is also using the Carrot (www.carrot.com) site. Luke and his company are doing the marketing right, with testimonials from people, actual videos, which greatly helps. He also has reviews, where he has pictures of houses that they have bought. This also shows the areas that they focus on. They also have great before and after pictures of the properties. I have not seen that before. So, I guess giving visitors an example of work they do. You will also see some frequently asked questions. This shows that they do a lot of online marketing.

We get a wide range of properties in varying conditions. From rundown to pristine — but always quality — houses.

**Ready to get in on the action?**

Click here for next steps

Michael from 416 Home Buyer is great too. He has videos to connect directly with the visitors as well as video testimonials. While they have a simple setup, Michael does a really good job with his website and it does not look like a Carrot site, but a custom-built website. He has "Contact Us" information and some connections to social media, as well as some examples of projects to sell. So, he has lots of connections here, and that picture of himself gets people to be familiar with him.

So, we have different examples of websites. Hopefully, you got a good idea of what is possible.

Now, if you use other services, you can help to legitimize your website, and it is a little trick that I have used. You can use services like Proof or Trust Pulse to let other visitors know that people are using your site. So, you actually use the power of association and that crowdsourcing to help you make connections with other people. This also adds authenticity to your offering, and it is a good way of showing testimonials and sharing information about your work and the team behind it.

**Danny Llaguno from Toronto, Ontario**
recently Joined/Renewed DurhamREI
4 hours ago   by TrustPulse

Essentially, it is more about creating that connection. So, if you look at DurhamREI.ca, you can see how I use it, when we have upcoming events, and then you will see people who have recently joined or renewed their DurhamREI membership. We can see where they are coming from and we are using that power. You can do the same thing for who submitted it. What was the name of the person that submitted it? Where did they submit it from? It can pop up on your screen. This greatly adds a boost to the authenticity of your business and shows that people are interested in your services.

## Advertising on Facebook or Google:

Some investors fill their lead funnels using adverts on social media sites, like Google and Facebook.

There is a higher cost to get involved with online advertising…but if you are tracking your online campaigns:

1. **You can see a correlation to actual properties that you buy, based on your advertising budget.**
2. **You can scale your advertising up or down depending on your needs.**

Some investors, all they do is use lead funnels and advertising on social media for all of their advertising. They do not do advertising, other than online. There are some higher costs involved. I know that people spend thousands a month on advertising. As long as you can correlate that to the actual properties being purchased, and based on your budget, you can scale it up or down depending on how busy you are. You will have to spend some time getting the hang of it.

If you are going to go down that path, Carrot has advertising services to help you with advertising, but you will have to spend some time learning this yourself or partnering with somebody familiar with it. This can be quite helpful for you. Lastly, I wanted to give you some action items to go and take a look at. You do not have to be an expert to start. Start by even putting twenty dollars in Facebook ads or Google to get some familiarity with the area and start talking to people. There are lots of resources on Google and Facebook about ads. Take a look at them and just get started.

Some places to learn more about advertising on Google is http://www.google.com/intl/en/ads/ and Facebook is https://www.facebook.com/about/ads/.

# Chapter 17

# Creating Equity from Emails.

We are still in marketing for off market properties, and this is still some pretty straightforward stuff. We are going to talk about creating equity from emails. I have also contacted landlords and property managers who are renting out properties on Kijiji and Craigslist. Usually, the way that I approach them is in two different ways. One is, *"Are you interested in selling your property?"* And the other one is, *"Are you interested in selling your property with your tenant there?"* That way, although it may be preferable for you not to, you still may be able to buy the property, especially if you are willing to take on the tenant. I found that it takes a lot of contacts before you get any leads generated and you annoy a few people who do not like it, but I call this process *"creating equity from emails."* It requires more determination to do. Instead of figuring out how you do it, you can find someone to do it for you.

So, the process is very simple. What you are doing is you are going to Kijiji or another rental reps website, and say something like, *"Are you interested in selling? I am an investor, I am not a realtor, I am looking for a rental property in the area, and I am willing to take on your existing tenants or vacant properties. Just let me know, Quentin."* That is it. You do not have a big ask or anything. All I am trying to do is to make a connection with people. I am trying to start conversations. From this, you know most of them are not going to go anywhere, but you will find the occasional one that takes you somewhere and that is the interesting part. All you really need to do is start.

Here is the response to the ads that I used:

*Are you interested in selling? I am an investor, not a realtor, and looking for a rental property in the area. I am willing to take on your existing tenants or vacant properties.*

*Let me know,*

*Quentin*

What I encourage you to do is when you read this chapter, go on to Kijiji. Now, take some time, look through it. See if there are any leads about homes that you would be interested in purchasing as an investor and contact the landlord or the property manager who is renting out the property and just ask. You will never know whether you can do something or not until you try it. It might make you uncomfortable and take you out of your comfort zone. Just remember, that is how you know you are growing.

# Chapter 18

# Dealing Directly with Potential Sellers.

This chapter is about "driving for dollars" or "door knocking for dollars," however you want to call it. If you want a deal, you are going to have to work with sellers directly, and that is going to be uncomfortable for some of you, especially if you are an introvert. Just remember, whenever you are doing something that takes you out of your comfort zone, you are growing and if you are not willing to do what others are willing to do, then you are not going to get what they are getting. If you want to work directly off the MLS and just buy off the MLS, then you do not have to worry about this, but we are talking about dealing directly with potential sellers.

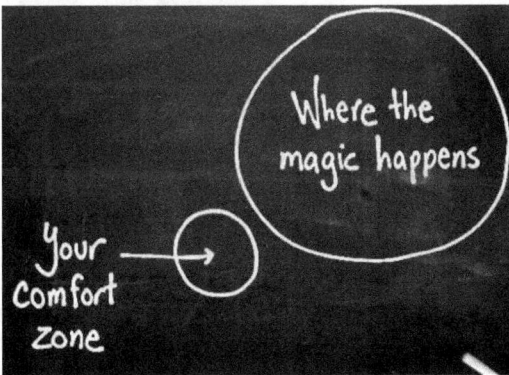

The first step you can take is door knocking. Whenever I have come across a property that looks rundown, I often see it as an opportunity to fix up the property. I would leave sticky notes, leave door hangers or just knock on the door, and let them know, *"I am interested in buying a property, if you are interested in selling, I am an investor in the area."* Make sure that they have a contact number so that they can get a hold of you. Just make sure that you have that connection.

*My name is John Smith
and I am interested in
buying this house. I am
not a realtor, I am
a contractor.*

*Please call me at
905-XXX-XXXX
if you are interested
in selling.*

Companies like Vistaprint make the process really straightforward. You can create the background of an image, put a sticky note on it, and then leave information. Here is an example: *"My name is an Al, I am interested in buying this house, I am not a realtor, I am not a contractor. Call me if you are interested in selling."* It does not have to be too crazy. It just has to excite or pique their interest to get somebody to call you and start that connection.

## Things to Look For:

- **Lawns are overgrown.**

- **Windows boarded up.**
- **Excess amount of newspapers/mail left at the front door.**
- **A mess of items on the front lawn.**
- **Lots of work needed on the outside of the house.**

What I am looking for when I am door knocking while driving for dollars: I try to spot overgrown lawns, boarded up windows, lots of newspapers left in the front, a mess of items on the lawn, work needed outside the house, etc. Sometimes, you cannot even tell because the outside of the house looks great but the inside is a hoarder house. That can be a bit tricky to do from the outside. If you are just generally focused on a specific area, you know that the rental properties make sense for a given street. Other people could be buying there, and then you are just door knocking on an entire street because it makes sense. It does not take much to get started, and then if nobody answers, you can leave them a sticky note on the door, talk to neighbors, and hand out business cards.

If you really want to get in there, go to the city and pull the land registry information on the property to contact the previous owner, whatever it takes. To find opportunities, sometimes you have to be more creative. Remember, spending this extra time will help you secure the deal.

## Getting Started:

- **Knocking on the door at first.**
- **Leave a sticky note on the door of the property.**
- **Talk to neighbors.**
- **Hand out business cards.**
- **Go to the city to pull the land registry information on a property to contact the previous owner.**

One of the things that you might look for is a big bin out in the front of the property…it is a good tell. It means that either they are going through some major renovations or they are cleaning out the property just before they are going to put it up for sale. This is a great one to leave a sticky note, especially if somebody's doing a big dump or garage sale. One thing I just want to remind you is that just because a property is cheap does not make it a good investment. I have found that sometimes you have a cheap property but it requires major renovations. The overall cost of the renovations does not make sense for the purchase of the property, especially when you are working in a competitive market. So, be careful that you are not overspending any savings that you receive based on the cost of the property.

In addition, you want to make sure that there is not any fire code or zoning issues, particularly if the house has grow-up or bylaw infractions. The cost to fix it would be thousands of dollars and can ruin your opportunity unless you buy it at a steep discount. You have to be sure of your numbers, and it is not something a new investor should start with. If you are going to find or get an opportunity like that, it is a good idea to bring an experienced investor to help you with such transactions.

# Cheap Does Not Always = Good Investment

# Chapter 19

# Leveraging Your Network

When I say leverage your network, I am talking about all parts of your network. You can talk to other investors and you can talk with other people. So, it can be difficult to describe but you send out a vibe to people whether you are confident or not around the type of properties you want to purchase and your ability to purchase something. You need to convey that to other people. If you want to start getting good deals, people need to know that you are not just a talker. You can close on a property and have funding financing in place. While it is important, you should be careful when making such commitments when you are starting out. Perhaps find partners that could help in the beginning.

Another thing is that there are other investors who make $200,000, $300,000, $400,000, or $500,000, and they are willing to give up $10,000 in equity because they believe that you are a good person and can help them in some other way. It could be closing the property in six months or twelve months from now, when they need to get it closed, because of tax reasons. Whatever it is, you want to find out what they need and try to help them. There could be a property management piece that you can help them with, and then they are willing to sell a property to you. Whatever that is, make sure that you stay in touch with those investors, and keep the door open and not burn any bridges.

Remember, especially if they are established real estate investors, you do not want to pester them all the time. You could contact them and see if they are interested in selling a property or two or their portfolio. Maybe they know somebody else who is selling a property. Stay in touch but do not bother them constantly. Do not start stalking their social media profiles, pinging, or instant messaging them. They get some weird people so just do not do that.

The other thing Is to develop relationships with builders and developers as well. They are a great source of unique opportunities for real estate investors, and some of them need to close a property quickly or they finished development and they just want to sell it quickly. This can be a great opportunity, as they can have several properties, and if you can buy a few of them when the numbers make sense, then you can take that off their hands at a discount. Develop those relationships, and as long as they create a win for the developer and builder, they would create a win for you. The idea is to find something that works for both of you.

You may also be interested in flipped properties. Oftentimes, when you talk to wholesalers, they take on single-family homes and convert them into duplexes or triplexes. Maybe you can create a win-win scenario with that flipper instead of them selling a property on the MLS and you can buy it directly from them. You do not need to use a realtor to go through the transaction, as long as you are happy with the quality of the house flipper, builder, or contractor. You still have to do your due diligence and have to do the proper paperwork. Make sure that they are not cutting corners on the bill or the general contracting piece. It could be a great opportunity, specifically dealing with being the end buyer for house flippers and then not having to worry about competition. Remember, this is leveraging the network that you either are developing or have developed.

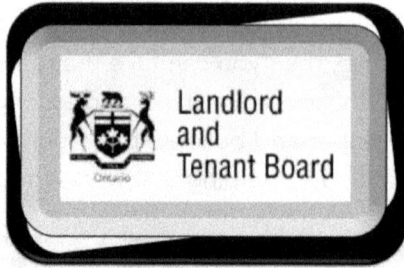

I have heard about people who place an ad for motivated sellers outside of the landlord-tenant board. Now, it is a little bit different, but if you are going in for cases being heard, you can post the signs out there.

Sometimes people would post signs for people who are going through a fire and flood outside of hotels, where people from insurance companies stay. You can also post signs around bankruptcy offices or check cashing offices to find motivated sellers. People do it in all kinds of places. It is about putting that information out there and giving them an option so that they can take advantage of it.

Chambers of Commerce, real estate club meetings, and meetup groups—talk about the type of properties that you are interested in and that you would pay for a referral. Let people know that you are buying properties at meetings, talk to people about what you are looking for, and there are meetings all across Canada. If you are not local to Durham, there are places in Vancouver, Victoria, and Ottawa where you can go meet other people and make deals happen—check out meeting websites like Meetup.com.

The other thing is that you want to pay for referrals. It is an easy way to create leads, create conversations with people, particularly subcontractors and professionals. Let them know, *"Hey, look, if you are interested and you find something that is an opportunity, I am happy to give you cash, like a bonus of 1 percent of what-ever the purchase price is, or whatever makes sense to you."* You can talk to property managers or contractors. It works, and I have done it before quite a few times. So, leverage your network, ask for referrals for properties that are closing, and then pay them for the referrals when you close on the property.

I have had contractors, property managers, and other investors give me leads about properties. So, make sure that you let your friends and family know that you are interested in purchasing real estate rental properties.

Keep in mind that there are a lot of people who deal with real estate on a day-to-day basis. Mortgage brokers, real estate lawyers, insurance agents, and bankers—you want to let those people know that you are looking for properties and you are willing to pay a referral fee. Talk to people that you generally socialize with. You do not have to make the conversation all about real estate talk, but casually bring it up in the conversation. You could be sitting with parents in the stands at your kid's sporting event, you talk about a property that you are working on, and then you let them know, *"Hey, look, if you know of any investment properties coming up, let me know, right, I will be really interested in purchasing it."* It is about having such conversations to help you to find the properties that you want.

Now, I have even had former tenants contact me about selling an off market property that they owned. They had a property that they wanted to sell from a family member, which had been inherited. It was a great way to connect with the potential seller. I was able to give the tenant a referral bonus, which actually came back to me in rent anyways. It is a great process because you never know where you are going to get your leads from.

Other people get in touch with different contractors, particularly in a disaster recovery or fire area. It can work as well, as long as you are purchasing it for the right price. While you can make a decent profit, they may require large-scale renovations, like a complete house tear down, so you have to be careful. You need to know what you are doing, and if you do not, you need to have a team that can help you to do it. That is something to be mindful of when it comes to these big projects but, again, there are plenty of opportunities for off market properties in this sector.

# Chapter 20

# Get Outside of the Box

We are going to look at some approaches and talk about the different pros and cons of using different marketing strategies. When it comes to finding discounted properties, just remember that there are various ways you could advertise to draw leads from sellers and bring them into the funnel. When people are employing different advertising approaches, it is often easy to give up or try something once and not be persistent. This is one of the causes of their failure. You also need to find the balance between the time it takes to use and do a strategy that actually generates leads as well as the costs associated with it. I would say that there is no single strategy that works better than the others. Generally, though sometimes you will find that one strategy works better in a particular area than different approaches, your job is to find out which one is going to work best for you in your area.

Make sure that you can scale and grow it, and you can generate the leads that you need for your business. There are many pros and cons of each strategy, and the only way for you to really know whether it is going to work is to implement it. You can talk with other real estate investors who are in the area and have tried different strategies. You will get their opinion, but it does not mean that you will have the same results as them. This is the real challenge when it comes to the different types of outside-the-box marketing.

All of these tactics will require you to contact the seller directly. You must have your voicemail system set up and your lead generation sheet ready to go. Make sure that you call them personally, especially if you are doing this for the first time. If you do have to go to the voicemail system, that voicemail system just confirms to the listener that they have contacted the right phone number and you need to get back to them right away. Make sure that you have all of those pieces set up before you start.

When you talk to the potential seller, you want to ensure that you get the key information. Keep it conversational, and do not bombard them with questions one after another but use your lead sheet to gather the information that you need. Remember, this process will essentially help you figure out whether you have a deal or not.

The other piece is that you will often run into people who have a lot of different issues. You need to remember that you are not a charity. I encourage you to give to charities and to give back, but it is not a good decision to purchase a property just to help somebody. It usually means that you are going to end up where you are crossing the line, and that is where some investors fail. They feel sorry for somebody, take on a project, and end up losing tens of thousands of dollars. While you should be empathetic towards people who have issues, you need to remember that at the end of the day, you are running a business, not a charity.

Finally, when you are doing any purchase, you will need to consider the seller's motivation. It is really crucial to figure out what they need and want, and how you can help them. If they are going through a foreclosure process and they need to close the property in ten days, solve the problem for them. Help them to do that and you will make it a win-win game. They will close the property in time and you will get the property at a discounted price, whatever that is. The second most important thing is to have different exit strategies on every single property you purchase.

Are you going to buy it yourself, flip it, hold it, or are you going to assign it to somebody else? Can you do a rent-to-own strategy on it? Whenever you are thinking, always have Plan B, Plan C—always have those other strategies in place so that you can quickly pivot from one to another. Remember, having a lead sheet that we talked about earlier, it becomes really important here that you have that filled out completely and you come up with your strategies and outline all of those things ahead of time.

## Consider the following on every purchase:

- **What is the seller's motivation?**
- **What are all the possible exit strategies on this property? (*You must have at least two—preferably three.*)**

# Chapter 21

# Car-Based Advertising

We are still thinking outside the box, and we are going to talk a little bit about car-based advertising. Yes, not something that everybody would want to try, but let us just talk about the options. I am putting it out because remember, this is thinking outside the box. There are different approaches to this. You can order car magnets from different companies like Vistaprint. They will stick on the sides of doors or trunks of vehicles, and they can easily be put on and taken off. The only thing about it is that it does look amateurish, but then again, it is nice to be able to take it on and off.

Another option is to do a car or truck wrap. Many companies offer this service across Canada, and you can search for a local company. In my area, we have a company that does car and truck wraps. I told my son that if he ever wants to get a car, I will give them one, but we will do bright yellow, **We Buy Houses** advertising wrap around the car. He has got a few years to go, but I think that might be interesting.

One of the things that you do want to consider, and there are some certain pros as well as cons to this:

## Pros

- **You are driving in the area where you are investing and people will see your signs.**
- **When you are parked, this could be a great conversation starter for potential sellers and perhaps even potential partners.**
- **If you are doing a wrap on your car, there is better potential to write off the vehicle in your taxes. (Talk to your tax accountant for specific advice and see if your car advertising would qualify.)**
- **Just make sure to talk to your accountant for advice around advertising and what that will look like.**

## Cons

- You are driving an advertisement. On the cool scale, this would be considered very uncool.

- You could attract unwanted attention from neighbors on potential properties that you are considering buying. They may see your car and ask the neighbor if they are selling their house and then you could have some instant competition.

- Do not ever think you will get away with a speeding ticket again—you stick out like a sore thumb.

- Insurance.

Ultimately, it is up to you, and it depends on where you are in life, especially on potential properties that you are considering buying. The other piece that you may want to consider is how that is going to affect your insurance as well. I think insurance is another piece that perhaps is not talked about a lot and I am just going to add it in here. It is definitely something to consider when you are doing this because it could affect your insurance rates, as now you are using something for business that is personal. Just a few pros and cons, and things to think about when you are doing this, and I want you to keep that in mind when you are thinking about these out-of-the-box strategies.

# Chapter 22

# Bandit Signs

There are lawn signs, and they are a great way to advertise locally. Do they work? Yes, they do. They are usually plastic or cardboard signs that you see sticking along with wood or metal spikes and advertise a product. You can buy the signs from various stores at a wide variety of costs. Some of them are plastic signs; some of them are almost like plastic, while some are corrugated cardboard. It is important, however, that whatever advertising you are using, you are tracking your responses to see if it is a worthwhile way of advertising. When someone calls your number, you always want to ask where they heard about your service, saw your sign, or got the information. I have even seen wholesalers use two different phone numbers and two different-looking signs that eventually go to the same place, so they essentially "create" their own competition. This is quite an interesting approach.

Earlier, we talked about Grasshopper and other online services to get multiple phone numbers. Well, you can use those multiple phone numbers to track where specific leads come from. You want to have a phone number that is easy to remember or a website address on your sign so that it is easy to follow up with you. Put these signs in areas that have quite a bit of car or foot traffic, as you want people to be able to remember your phone number.

This sign is a great example because it has bright pink colors and white contrast, but I think it also appeals to different people. Remember to have phone numbers and repeat those phone numbers again and again, on different advertisements. Remember, contrast helps people see exactly what you want them to see easily when you are driving by. You also want to map out or write down where you are placing your signs so that you can track the results. People often hire somebody to go out and place their signs at designated locations. You can easily track them down and see where these signs are going. If you bought 100 signs, you could hire somebody to put up those 100 signs and you would just have to indicate on the map where you want them to go.

I recommend that if you are going to be doing bandit signs, make sure to do the tracking. This can be done by having unique signs or phone numbers. I would suggest that you should mix things up so that you can assess what is working and what is not.

You can post an ad on places like Craigslist and Kijiji, asking for someone who can post the signs in different areas. The idea here is that when you grab somebody to help you from Kijiji or Craigslist, you are not doing that ten dollar an hour job yourself. You are working towards earning the thousands of dollars that come from talking to a potential seller and getting the deal under contract. That is why you want to use these types of online services to help you. You can also post your "We Buy Houses" on online sites like this. I just think that for now, for bandit signs, it makes a lot of sense to hire somebody using those services. You can try a couple of streets first to see what the results are before expanding to the rest of the area.

## Pros

- **You can advertise in a specific area or even on specific streets.**
- **You inspire lots of curiosity from people—especially if you use a hand-drawn sign.**

Some of the pros of this are that you can advertise in a specific area or specific streets. You get a lot of curiosity from people in particular if you have hand-drawn signs, although it takes a lot of extra work, it might be worth the effort. You can post them on different street signs or streetlight posts. Those are often good sports, where you see a lot of those bandit signs go up.

## Cons

- **Someone will need to put up the signs and take them down if necessary. This can be very time intensive.**
- **Someone needs to purchase the signs (can cost money) and/or create the signs (can be time intensive).**
- **Your city or town will have specific rules when it comes to bandit signs and advertisements.**
- **Some places will even charge you a fine for each sign that you put out. So, you should know the local bylaws and avoid having to be corrected by the city or town.**

There are also a few places you need to put the signs up but then take them down at a specific time. They can go up on Friday night but they have to come down on Sunday night and that can be very time intensive. To avoid this, you need to be familiar with the local bylaws or you will be corrected by the city or town, often with a fine, and it is usually a fine for each sign that you have.

Additionally, someone will need to purchase, organize, create, and post the signs. It can be quite a time intensive activity. Those are some things that you want to think about when you are going to be using bandit signs as part of your out-of-the-box advertising campaign.

# Chapter 23

# Stickers

Stickers are a great alternative to bandit signs as they can be ordered quite inexpensively from various printing stores. There are a few key things to consider when it comes to stickers. Make sure that the sticker sticks really well. They should be easy to read, have high contrast, visible phone numbers, and be catchy. You want the number to be noticeable to people driving by. Most people like to use yellow and black, but it is great to differentiate your sticker, so try something along the lines of lime green or pink background with black font. Whatever you use, with regards to the stickers, they should be clearly visible when you are driving by. That is the key especially since a lot of people like to put stickers on surfaces around areas that people frequently visit.

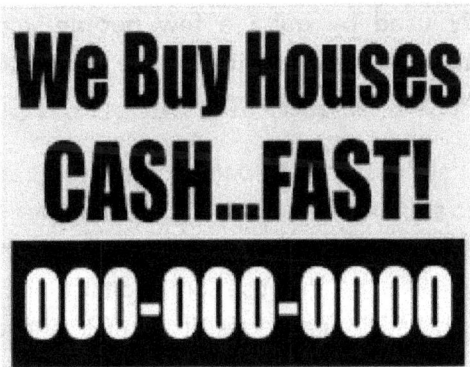

## We Buy Houses CASH...FAST! 000-000-0000

For instance, turning left, as you have enough time when you are turning left to see the sign and note down the number. So, that is something you will have to consider with this mode of advertising. Stickers can be ordered in bulk, and then you can use them or post them in a lot of different spots. They are a low-cost, quick-to-install option, and you can paste them at creative locations, such as behind street signs and street posts. You can get plastic-coated stickers that stay up for longer and they are harder to remove.

## Pros

- **Relatively economical and quick to install.**
- **Creative locations where the stickers can be posted—behind street signs on street posts.**
- **You can get plastic-coated stickers that are easy to read for a long time.**

Some of the cons just like in bandit signs, you have to be careful with regards to local bylaws and it can be time intensive.

## Cons

- **Can be a time-intensive activity and may require you to outsource to someone.**
- **Already used by quite a few people and when you advertise the same service beside someone else's sign, they can get really upset.**

However, as I suggested with bandit signs, you can use Kijiji to outsource it to someone. Another thing is that when other people are offering similar services, they may not want your stickers over or near their stickers. It can cause some conflict, and I have heard of people facing such challenges. It is important to investigate what is already working and what is already being done in your area. This will make it a lot easier for you to do stickers or any other marketing campaign. If you find that some did the sticker campaigns before you but are not doing it anymore, then perhaps you should probe further to find out why they gave up. In any case, putting those stickers and getting them out there can be a great way of spreading awareness about your marketing.

# Chapter 24

# Door Hangers,
# Flyers, or Postcards

Door hangers, flyers, or postcards, however you want to look at it, are also nifty marketing tools. There are lots of different types and ways to use them. I have seen them broadly distributed to people in different areas. This is different from perhaps a letter campaign. We are usually using a delivery service, something like Five Star Distribution out in the Durham area or Canada Post focused on postal codes.

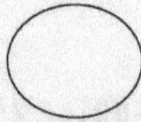

# Need to Sell Fast?
# We Buy Houses
# CASH

**In Pickering, Ajax, Whitby ...**

Dear Homeowner,

We buy houses from people in situations just like yours in almost any area or price range. We specialize in finding creative solutions to real estate problems others won't touch. We can close quickly.

We are not Realtors. We are real estate investors, who want to buy your house.

Find out how we can put your real estate headaches behind you.

P.S. Rarely do problems just go away. Call now, let's find a solution for you.

Call John at **1-xxx-xxx-xxx**

### Typical Problems We Solve:

- ☑ Divorce?
- ☑ Loss of Job?
- ☑ Inheritance?
- ☑ Need Repairs?
- ☑ Tired Landlord?
- ☑ Bankruptcy?
- ☑ Bad Tenants?
- ☑ Can't Afford Payments?
- ☑ Two House Payments?
- ☑ Can't Maintain House?
- ☑ Need to Move Now?
- ☑ About to be Foreclosed?
- ☑ Expired Listing?
- ☑ Need Cash?

**Get a FREE - No Obligation - No Risk Assessment of Your Current Situation**
**\*\*STOP Foreclosure/Power of Sale\*\***
**Call Now 1-XXX-XXX-XXXX**

**www.xxxxx.ca**

Alternatively, if you are trying to save money, you can look at Kijiji and Craigslist to see if you can find some locals who are interested in doing such deliveries for you. From a reliability perspective, however, it is usually a lot better to use Canada Post or a distribution service that will usually charge you per 1,000 deliveries depending on what you are trying to achieve, and usually, if you do more, you stand to save more. The key with a lot of these types of advertising is consistency. You cannot just do it once, as you have to do at least three to twelve months. You want to have consistency, and you want to be able to track if the leads are coming from that advertising.

I have seen door hangers work in specific areas, and then eventually it does not work anymore, and then I have seen online advertising work really well in an area, and then not working as well as a letter campaign. All of this is a bit of trial and error, but again, being able to use something like this to advertise can help bring you leads. You can have more time, share more information, and speak to different types of audiences when you are using them.

## Pros

- **Can have more time, share more information, and speak to different audiences.**
- **There are plenty of established printing services and delivery options that you can leverage.**

There are lots of printing and delivery services in the market, and you can establish leverage quickly as you have a plethora of options to choose from.

As for cons, you might not like the property type that this approach attracts. The cost of printing and delivery can add up, especially in large areas. How many flyers, postcards, and door hangers do you just throw away without looking at them? You can imagine that there is going to be a lot of that happening with yours as well. You want to keep that in mind.

## Cons

- **You might not like the types of properties that this advertising attracts or the areas that you get leads from.**
- **The cost of printing and the delivery costs increase when you scale up.**
- **How many flyers/postcards/door hangers do you throw away without even looking at them?**

Moreover, with all of this type of direct-to-seller advertising, be prepared for irrelevant messages and people calling the police. These things happen, as well, so you will need to develop a thick skin. Door hangers, flyers, and postcards can look a little different, but lots of great places to get that done for you and just another out-of-the-box strategy for you to experiment with.

# Chapter 25

# Business Cards

We are still on the subject of thinking outside the box. Business cards are an easy way to let people know the type of services that you offer. Spend a few extra dollars and make them a bit appealing instead of the monotone generic cards. You can leave business cards in all sorts of places—on service boards, restaurants, stores, beside urinals, wherever you want to put them. You can use business cards in different ways—you can leave in club meetings and networking events. You can leave them with people, however you want to do it. One of the things you may want to include is a separate business card that you just give to traders and you add the referral information, like "*I give a $1,000 referral bonus to any property that we close on.*"

As for the pros of business cards, they are relatively inexpensive and easy to produce. You can get them done almost anywhere and they add a credibility factor. Particularly if you are going to use contact information that has a professional look—a 1-800 number with a local number, and maybe a URL that is not a Gmail account. They are small and easy for sellers to keep. You have a lot of space to convey messages, especially if you use a double card, and you flip open and you use the inside of it. There is a lot of "*real estate*" that you can take up with your message in there.

We Buy Houses
CASH

Any Price - Any Area - Any Condition

www.XXXXXXX.ca

XXX-XXX-XXXX

Call Us Today For A No Obligation CASH Offer

Divorce?
Can't Afford Payments?
Loss of Job?
Making Two House Payments?
Inheritance?
Need Repairs?
Can't Maintain the House?
Tired Landlord?
Need to Move Immediately?
Bankruptcy?
About to be in Foreclosure?
Bad Tenants?
Expired Listing?
Need Cash?

WE CAN
HELP!

We are not Realtors.
We are Real Estate Investors,
who wants to buy your house.
Call now to find out how we
can put your real estate
headaches behind you.

Let's find a solution for you.

## Pros

- These are relatively low priced and easy to produce.
- They give you a little more credibility, especially if you can include the different associations that you belong to.
- They are small and easy for sellers to keep.
- You have more space to convey your message.

Some of the cons are that it is easy to lose a business card. They are sometimes too small and easy to ignore.

## Cons

- It is easy to lose a business card.
- It is small and easy to ignore.

You can also have a business card, specifically for your off market purchases. You should consider this as a tool and I would recommend it as well, as you can use a lot of different services to get these cards. You can use the example that I have there to get you started, but you can also just Google "We Buy Houses Business Cards" and you will get a ton of different examples to look at as well.

# Chapter 26

# Other Ideas

We are wrapping up the "*thinking outside the box*" with some pretty outside-the-box stuff here. Dialling for dollars is going directly to "for sale by owner" signs, contacting the seller using contact phone numbers, you can find the motivation of the seller, and see whether it really is an opportunity to solve a problem, or are they just looking to get the most money possible.

## Dialing for Dollars

Whenever I see a number on a "*for sale by owner*" sign, I will try to contact the seller directly using a contact phone number. This enables me to find out the motivation of the seller and really see if there is an opportunity to solve the problem. One of the things that I want to try in the future is to contact landlords who have rental ads posted on online rental websites.

You can also contact landlords on rental property as well as websites and contact them directly. Talk to them directly. Find out if they are interested in selling their properties or if there is something that you can do to solve the problem. Try to create a relationship with them, and maybe in the future, they will want to contact you to sell a property.

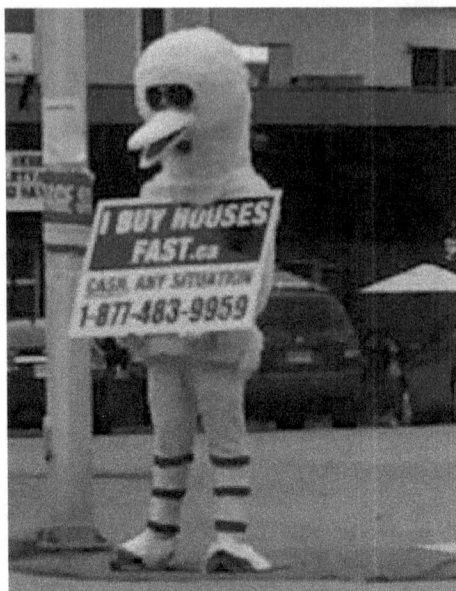

## Walking Billboard

This is a way out there idea, but yes, that is someone in a costume standing on the corner of a street in Hamilton, with an "I Buy Houses" sign!

This one is a pretty unique approach and it is without a doubt grabbing attention. This phone number is probably on a handful of different people's websites and shared with different people. It is just different and eye-catching.

You can use your creativity here, just make sure it is legal, but remember, the idea is that you want people to phone you—good or bad. You will have lots of different phone numbers for people who phone you, but the idea is that you are connecting with more sellers and that those sellers are going to lead to off market purchases. Being creative and doing unique things to drive those leads in will help you to close more deals.

# Chapter 27

# Conclusion

Overall, there is huge potential for real estate investors in off market properties. In addition to less competition, flexible negotiations, and higher profit margins, off market real estate is worth focusing your time on. Despite them not being listed on the MLS, I shared a vast array of approaches and marketing tactics that beginners can employ to generate off market real estate leads and close those deals. I recommend testing out the different strategies mentioned in this book on a smaller scale first, while having a system to keep track of the leads that come in. This will help you figure out which approaches work best in your area of interest so that you can scale up from there and achieve your real estate dream.

If you enjoyed this book and you are looking for more depth, there is a video course available at **www.FindingDiscounted-Properties.com**.

When you register, you will be able to access a number of documents and agreements that were mentioned in this book, that I have literally spent tens of thousands of dollars on over the years.

Visit **www.FindingDiscountedProperties.com** for more details and join today.

# Suggested Reading

Conti, Peter. *Making Big Money Investing in Foreclosures without Cash or Credit.* Kaplan Pub., 2007.

Esajian, Paul. *The Real Estate Rehab Investing Bible.* John Wiley & Sons Inc., 2014.

Ferrazzi, Keith, and Tahl Raz. *Never Eat Alone, Expanded and Updated and Other Secrets to Success, One Relationship at a Time.* Portfolio Penguin, 2014.

Finkel, David, and Peter Conti. *Buying Real Estate without Cash or Credit.* John Wiley & Sons, 2005.

Klaff, Oren. *Pitch Anything an Innovative Method for Presenting, Persuading and Winning the Deal.* McGraw-Hill, 2011.

LeGrand, Ron. *How to Be a Quick Turn Real Estate Millionaire: Make Fast Cash with No Money, Credit, or Previous Experience.* Dearborn Trade Pub., 2004.

Mackay, Harvey. *Dig Your Well before You're Thirsty: The Only Networking Book You'll Ever Need.* Currency/Doubleday, 1999.

Merrill, Than. *The Real Estate Wholesaling Bible: The Fastest, Easiest Way to Get Started in Real Estate Investing.* Wiley, 2014.

Myers, Kevin C. *Buy It, Fix It, Sell It: Profit!* Dearborn Trade, 2003.

Ono, July. *Your Million Dollar Network: How to Start and Build Your Million Dollar Network.* On the Beach Education Corp., 2008.

Scott, J., et al. *The Book on Negotiating Real Estate: Expert Strategies for Getting the Best Deals When Buying & Selling Investment Property.* 1-2-3 Flip Press, 2017.

# Author Biography – Quentin D'Souza

Quentin D'Souza is a multiple award-winning Real Estate Investor, and a trusted authority on real estate investing. He is an Ontario Certified Teacher and holds two university degrees, which includes a Master's in Education. Quentin has appeared on local and national television and radio, interviewed in national publications, and has been a keynote speaker to large audiences of real estate investors.

Quentin is a proud member of the Entrepreneurs' Organization. His company, Appleridge Homes, uses the Buy, Fix, Refinance, and Rent strategy on long-term rental properties in Ontario, Canada, as well as with joint venture partnerships to create win/win relationships on Apartment Building purchases. Quentin owns a real estate portfolio in excess of $80 million dollars of assets under management across Canada and the US and transacted on 80+ properties since 2004.

Quentin is a trusted authority on the Durham Real Estate Market and has worked with and mentored thousands of real estate investors through the Durham Real Estate Investor Club at www. DurhamREI.ca, since 2008, and the Real Estate Investors Video Training Site at www.EducationREI.ca.

Quentin is also the author of *The Property Management Toolbox: A How-To Guide for Ontario Real Estate Investors and Landlords* and *The Filling Vacancies Toolbox: A Step-By-Step Guide for Ontario Real Estate Investors and Landlords for Renting Out Residential Real Estate* (www.TheOntarioLandlordToolbox.ca), which are comprehensive guides for getting a real estate business going. He is a coauthor of *The Ultimate Wealth Strategy: Your Complete Guide to Buying, Fixing, Refinancing, and Renting Real Estate* (www.theultimatewealthstrategy.com), which shares his strategy for building a real estate portfolio. Quentin published *The Action Taker's lic Planner* (www.actiontakerrealestateplanner. com), a goal attainment tool for real estate investors. He has also published "The Scaling Up Toolbox: A How to Guide for Real Estate Investors Who Don't Have to Use Their Own Money to Buy Property," a roadmap to help build your real estate investing system.

Quentin manages a large real estate portfolio and works with other investors using joint ventures through his company, Appleridge Homes.

You can also listen to his podcast at www.GetRealWealthy.com and can be contacted at quentin@getrealwealthy.com.

Quentin can often be found at one of his two sons' sports events or activities. When you see him in the community, please introduce yourself.

www.ingramcontent.com/pod-product-compliance
Lightning Source LLC
Chambersburg PA
CBHW071225210326
41597CB00016B/1946